AZURE NETWORKING

COMMAND LINE MASTERY
FROM BEGINNER TO ARCHITECT

4 BOOKS IN 1

BOOK 1
AZURE NETWORKING ESSENTIALS: A BEGINNER'S GUIDE TO COMMAND LINE BASICS

BOOK 2
MASTERING AZURE CLI: INTERMEDIATE TECHNIQUES FOR NETWORKING IN THE CLOUD

BOOK 3
ADVANCED AZURE NETWORKING: OPTIMIZING PERFORMANCE AND SECURITY WITH CLI MASTERY

BOOK 4
AZURE NETWORKING ARCHITECT: EXPERT STRATEGIES AND BEST PRACTICES FOR CLI POWER USERS

ROB BOTWRIGHT

Published by Rob Botwright
Library of Congress Cataloging-in-Publication Data
ISBN 978-1-83938-770-8
Cover design by Rizzo

Disclaimer

The contents of this book are based on extensive research and the best available historical sources. However, the author and publisher make no claims, promises, or guarantees about the accuracy, completeness, or adequacy of the information contained herein. The information in this book is provided on an "as is" basis, and the author and publisher disclaim any and all liability for any errors, omissions, or inaccuracies in the information or for any actions taken in reliance on such information. The opinions and views expressed in this book are those of the author and do not necessarily reflect the official policy or position of any organization or individual mentioned in this book. Any reference to specific people, places, or events is intended only to provide historical context and is not intended to defame or malign any group, individual, or entity. The information in this book is intended for educational and entertainment purposes only. It is not intended to be a substitute for professional advice or judgment. Readers are encouraged to conduct their own research and to seek professional advice where appropriate. Every effort has been made to obtain necessary permissions and acknowledgments for all images and other copyrighted material used in this book. Any errors or omissions in this regard are unintentional, and the author and publisher will correct them in future editions.

BOOK 1 - AZURE NETWORKING ESSENTIALS: A BEGINNER'S GUIDE TO COMMAND LINE BASICS

BOOK 2 - MASTERING AZURE CLI: INTERMEDIATE TECHNIQUES FOR NETWORKING IN THE CLOUD

BOOK 3 - ADVANCED AZURE NETWORKING: OPTIMIZING PERFORMANCE AND SECURITY WITH CLI MASTERY

BOOK 4 - AZURE NETWORKING ARCHITECT: EXPERT STRATEGIES AND BEST PRACTICES FOR CLI POWER USERS

Introduction

Welcome to the "Azure Networking Command Line Mastery" book bundle, where you will embark on a journey from beginner to architect level proficiency in managing Azure networking environments using the Command Line Interface (CLI). This comprehensive bundle consists of four books, each designed to equip you with the essential knowledge and skills needed to excel in Azure networking.

In Book 1, "Azure Networking Essentials: A Beginner's Guide to Command Line Basics," you will start your journey by learning the foundational concepts of Azure networking and mastering the basics of the Azure CLI. From creating virtual networks to configuring network security groups, this book will lay the groundwork for your understanding of Azure networking fundamentals.

Building upon your beginner-level skills, Book 2, "Mastering Azure CLI: Intermediate Techniques for Networking in the Cloud," will take you deeper into the world of Azure networking. You will explore intermediate-level techniques for managing Azure networking resources, including virtual network peering, Azure DNS configuration, and virtual network gateway deployment.

As you progress to Book 3, "Advanced Azure Networking: Optimizing Performance and Security with CLI Mastery," you will dive into advanced optimization strategies and security best practices for Azure networking. Discover how to optimize network performance, implement granular security policies, and leverage advanced features like Azure Firewall and Application Gateway.

Finally, in Book 4, "Azure Networking Architect: Expert Strategies and Best Practices for CLI Power Users," you will reach the pinnacle of your Azure networking journey. Here, you will learn expert-level strategies and best practices for designing and architecting Azure networking solutions. From designing redundant and highly available network architectures to enforcing governance policies, this book will equip you with the knowledge and skills needed to excel as a CLI power user and network architect.

Whether you are just starting your journey in Azure networking or aiming to become an expert in CLI-powered networking solutions, this book bundle provides a comprehensive roadmap to help you achieve your goals. Get ready to master Azure networking through CLI mastery and unlock the full potential of your cloud infrastructure.

BOOK 1
AZURE NETWORKING ESSENTIALS
A BEGINNER'S GUIDE TO COMMAND LINE BASICS
ROB BOTWRIGHT

Chapter 1: Understanding Azure Networking Fundamentals

Azure Networking Components encompass a diverse array of services and features within the Azure cloud ecosystem, each playing a crucial role in enabling robust and scalable networking solutions for businesses of all sizes. At the core of Azure Networking lies the Virtual Network (VNet), a fundamental building block that allows users to provision and manage private networks in the cloud. VNets provide isolation and segmentation for resources deployed within Azure, offering a secure environment for workloads and applications. Within a VNet, subnets further divide the network into smaller segments, allowing for more granular control over network traffic and resource placement. This hierarchical structure enables organizations to design and implement complex network architectures tailored to their specific requirements. Additionally, Azure offers a range of connectivity options to bridge on-premises environments with the cloud, including Virtual Network Gateways, VPN (Virtual Private Network) connections, and Azure ExpressRoute. These services facilitate seamless integration between Azure resources and existing infrastructure, enabling hybrid networking scenarios that combine the flexibility of the cloud with the control of on-premises environments. Azure Networking also includes advanced networking features such as Network Security Groups (NSGs) and Azure Firewall, which provide robust network security capabilities. NSGs allow users to define inbound and outbound traffic rules, effectively controlling access to resources based on source and destination IP addresses, ports, and protocols. Azure Firewall, on the other hand, is a managed, cloud-based network security service that provides stateful firewall capabilities and application-level filtering for inbound and outbound traffic. Together, these services help organizations enforce security policies and protect their assets from unauthorized access and malicious threats. In addition to security, Azure Networking offers comprehensive monitoring and troubleshooting capabilities to ensure the reliability and performance of network resources. Azure Monitor provides centralized monitoring and logging for Azure services, allowing users to collect and analyze telemetry data from various sources, including virtual machines, virtual networks, and network security groups. With Azure Network Watcher, users can diagnose and troubleshoot network connectivity issues, perform packet captures, and analyze network traffic flows. These tools enable proactive monitoring and rapid resolution of network-related issues, minimizing downtime and ensuring a seamless user experience. As organizations continue to migrate their workloads to the cloud and adopt hybrid cloud architectures, the importance of robust and reliable networking solutions cannot be overstated. Azure Networking Components provide the foundation for building scalable, secure, and high-performance networks in the cloud, empowering businesses to innovate and grow with confidence. Whether deploying applications globally, connecting distributed environments, or securing critical workloads, Azure Networking offers a comprehensive suite of services and features to meet the most demanding networking requirements. Understanding network topologies in Azure is essential for designing and deploying scalable, reliable, and secure cloud-based infrastructures. At its core, a network topology refers to the layout or structure of a network, including the arrangement of its nodes, connections, and communication paths. In Azure, several network topologies are commonly used to meet different business requirements and architectural goals. One of the most fundamental network topologies in Azure is the hub-and-spoke model, which provides a centralized hub (or core) network that connects to multiple spoke networks. This topology is well-suited for organizations with a centralized IT infrastructure that need to connect multiple branch offices, departments, or business units. In the hub-and-spoke model, the hub network serves as a central point for managing network traffic, enforcing security policies, and providing connectivity to other networks. Spoke networks, on the other hand, are connected to the hub network and typically represent individual business units, applications, or workloads. This hierarchical structure allows for centralized management and control while providing isolation and segmentation between different parts of the organization. Another common network topology in Azure is the peer-to-peer (P2P) model, also known as a mesh topology. In a P2P topology, each node in the network is connected to every other node, forming a fully interconnected network. This topology is well-suited for scenarios where every node needs to communicate directly with every other node, such as peer-to-peer file sharing or real-time collaboration applications. While the P2P model offers maximum flexibility and redundancy, it can also be more complex to manage and scale, especially as the number of nodes in the network grows. Azure also supports hybrid network topologies that combine on-premises infrastructure with cloud-based resources. For example, organizations can use Azure Virtual Network Gateways to establish secure VPN connections between their on-premises networks and Azure VNets. This allows them to extend their existing network infrastructure into the cloud, enabling seamless communication between on-premises and cloud-based resources. Additionally, Azure ExpressRoute provides dedicated, private connectivity to Azure over a high-speed, low-latency connection, bypassing the public internet. This is particularly useful for organizations with stringent security and compliance requirements or high-bandwidth *workloads that require predictable performance. When designing network topologies in Azure, it's important to consider factors such as scalability, performance, security, and cost. By understanding the strengths and weaknesses of different network topologies and selecting the right one for their specific requirements, organizations can build robust and efficient cloud-based infrastructures that meet their business needs. Furthermore, Azure provides a range of networking services and features to help organizations implement and manage complex network topologies effectively. These include virtual networks, subnets, network security groups, load balancers, application gateways, and more. By leveraging these services, organizations can create resilient, high-performance networks that support their applications and workloads with ease. In summary, understanding network topologies in Azure is crucial for architecting successful cloud-based solutions. Whether deploying a hub-and-spoke, peer-to-peer, or hybrid topology, organizations must carefully consider their requirements and choose the right topology to meet their needs. With Azure's robust networking capabilities and services, organizations can build secure, scalable, and reliable networks that drive business innovation and growth.*

Chapter 2: Introduction to Azure Command Line Interface (CLI)

Installing and Configuring Azure CLI is a fundamental step for developers, system administrators, and DevOps engineers seeking to leverage the power of the command line interface for managing Azure resources efficiently and effectively. To begin the process, users need to ensure they have a compatible operating system, as Azure CLI is supported on various platforms including Windows, macOS, and Linux. For Windows users, the installation process involves downloading and running the Azure CLI installer from the official Microsoft website, while macOS users can install Azure CLI using Homebrew or MacPorts package managers. Linux users, depending on their distribution, can install Azure CLI using package managers such as apt, yum, or zypper. Once installed, users can open a command prompt or terminal window to start using Azure CLI. The first step in configuring Azure CLI is to authenticate with an Azure account, which can be done using the az login command. This command prompts users to open a browser window where they can sign in with their Azure credentials and authorize Azure CLI to access their account. Once authenticated, users can begin interacting with Azure resources using Azure CLI commands. Azure CLI commands follow a simple syntax structure, consisting of the az keyword followed by a command group, subcommand, and optional parameters. For example, to list all the virtual machines in an Azure subscription, users can use the az vm list command. Similarly, to create a new virtual machine, users can use the az vm create command, providing the necessary parameters such as resource group name, virtual machine name, and image name. Azure CLI also supports tab completion, which allows users to quickly navigate and autocomplete commands and parameters by pressing the Tab key. This feature enhances productivity and reduces the likelihood of typographical errors when working with complex commands. In addition to basic command execution, Azure CLI provides powerful features for scripting and automation, allowing users to streamline repetitive tasks and workflows. By combining Azure CLI commands with shell scripting languages such as Bash or PowerShell, users can automate the provisioning, configuration, and management of Azure resources. For example, users can create scripts to deploy entire infrastructure environments, configure network settings, or manage virtual machines at scale. Azure CLI also offers support for Azure Resource Manager (ARM) templates, which are JSON files that define the desired state of Azure resources and their configurations. Users can use Azure CLI commands such as az group deployment create to deploy ARM templates, providing the template file and parameter values as inputs. This approach enables infrastructure as code (IaC) practices, allowing users to version-control their infrastructure configurations and deploy them consistently across different environments. Furthermore, Azure CLI provides extensive documentation and built-in help features to assist users in learning and mastering its capabilities. Users can use the az -h command to display help information for Azure CLI, including available commands, subcommands, and parameters. Additionally, Azure CLI documentation is available online, providing detailed explanations, examples, and best practices for using Azure CLI commands effectively. Users can refer to the documentation to learn about specific features, troubleshoot issues, or explore advanced usage scenarios. Overall, Installing and Configuring Azure CLI is a foundational skill for anyone working with Azure cloud services, offering a versatile and efficient way to manage Azure resources from the command line. By mastering Azure CLI, users can streamline their workflows, automate repetitive tasks, and unlock the full potential of the Azure cloud platform for their projects and initiatives. Installing and Configuring Azure CLI is a fundamental step for developers, system administrators, and DevOps engineers seeking to leverage the power of the command line interface for managing Azure resources efficiently and effectively. To begin the process, users need to ensure they have a compatible operating system, as Azure CLI is supported on various platforms including Windows, macOS, and Linux. For Windows users, the installation process involves downloading and running the Azure CLI installer from the official Microsoft website, while macOS users can install Azure CLI using Homebrew or MacPorts package managers. Linux users, depending on their distribution, can install Azure CLI using package managers such as apt, yum, or zypper. Once installed, users can open a command prompt or terminal window to start using Azure CLI. The first step in configuring Azure CLI is to authenticate with an Azure account, which can be done using the az login command. This command prompts users to open a browser window where they can sign in with their Azure credentials and authorize Azure CLI to access their account. Once authenticated, users can begin interacting with Azure resources using Azure CLI commands. Azure CLI commands follow a simple syntax structure, consisting of the az keyword followed by a command group, subcommand, and optional parameters. For example, to list all the virtual machines in an Azure subscription, users can use the az vm list command. Similarly, to create a new virtual machine, users can use the az vm create command, providing the necessary parameters such as resource group name, virtual machine name, and image name. Azure CLI also supports tab completion, which allows users to quickly navigate and autocomplete commands and parameters by pressing the Tab key. This feature enhances productivity and reduces the likelihood of typographical errors when working with complex commands. In addition to basic command execution, Azure CLI provides powerful features for scripting and automation, allowing users to streamline repetitive tasks and workflows. By combining Azure CLI commands with shell scripting languages such as Bash or PowerShell, users can automate the provisioning, configuration, and management of Azure resources. For example, users can create scripts to deploy entire infrastructure environments, configure network settings, or manage virtual machines at scale. Azure CLI also offers support for Azure Resource Manager (ARM) templates, which are JSON files that define the desired state of Azure resources and their configurations. Users can use Azure CLI commands such as az group deployment create to deploy ARM templates, providing the template file and parameter values as inputs. This approach enables infrastructure as code (IaC) practices, allowing users to version-control their infrastructure configurations and deploy them consistently across different environments. Furthermore, Azure CLI provides extensive documentation and built-in help features to assist users in learning and mastering its capabilities. Users can use the az -h command to display help information for Azure CLI, including available commands, subcommands, and parameters. Additionally, Azure CLI documentation is available online, providing detailed explanations, examples, and best practices for using Azure CLI commands effectively. Users can refer to the documentation to learn about specific features, troubleshoot issues, or explore advanced usage scenarios. Overall, Installing and Configuring Azure CLI is a foundational skill for anyone working with Azure cloud services, offering a versatile and efficient way to manage Azure resources from the command line. By mastering Azure CLI, users can streamline their workflows, automate repetitive tasks, and unlock the full potential of the Azure cloud platform for their projects and initiatives.

Chapter 3: Setting Up Your Azure Networking Environment

Creating Virtual Networks (VNets) in Azure is a foundational step in building cloud-based infrastructures that provide secure and isolated communication between virtual machines (VMs), services, and resources. To create a VNet using Azure CLI, users can use the az network vnet create command, specifying parameters such as resource group name, VNet name, and address space. For example, the command az network vnet create --resource-group MyResourceGroup --name MyVNet --address-prefixes 10.0.0.0/16 creates a VNet named "MyVNet" with the address space 10.0.0.0/16 in the resource group "MyResourceGroup". When creating a VNet, users can also define subnets within the VNet to segment network traffic and isolate resources. This can be done using the az network vnet subnet create command, specifying parameters such as VNet name, subnet name, and address prefix. For example, the command az network vnet subnet create --resource-group MyResourceGroup --vnet-name MyVNet --name MySubnet --address-prefixes 10.0.0.0/24 creates a subnet named "MySubnet" with the address prefix 10.0.0.0/24 in the VNet "MyVNet" within the resource group "MyResourceGroup". By creating multiple subnets within a VNet, users can segment their *network into logical units and apply different network policies and security rules to each subnet. Additionally, users can configure network security groups (NSGs) to control inbound and outbound traffic to and from resources within the VNet. NSGs act as a basic firewall, allowing users to define rules that permit or deny traffic based on source and destination IP addresses, ports, and protocols. NSGs can be associated with subnets or individual network interfaces attached to VMs within the VNet, providing granular control over network traffic. To create an NSG using Azure CLI, users can use the az network nsg create command, specifying parameters such as resource group name and NSG name. For example, the command az network nsg create --resource-group MyResourceGroup --name MyNSG creates an NSG named "MyNSG" in the resource group "MyResourceGroup". Once created, users can define inbound and outbound security rules for the NSG using the az network nsg rule create command. For example, the command az network nsg rule create --resource-group MyResourceGroup --nsg-name MyNSG --name AllowSSH --protocol Tcp --direction Inbound --priority 100 --source-address-prefixes '*' --source-port-ranges '*' --destination-address-prefixes '*' --destination-port-ranges 22 --access Allow creates a security rule named "AllowSSH" that allows inbound SSH traffic (port 22) from any source to any destination. In addition to subnets and NSGs, users can also configure route tables within a VNet to* control the flow of network traffic within the VNet and to external destinations. Route tables allow users to define routes that specify where traffic should be directed based on destination IP addresses. For example, users can create a route table that directs traffic destined for a specific IP range to a virtual appliance or network virtual appliance (NVA) for further processing or inspection. Route tables can be associated with subnets within the VNet using the az network vnet subnet update command. For example, the command az network vnet subnet update --resource-group MyResourceGroup --vnet-name MyVNet --name MySubnet --route-table MyRouteTable associates the route table "MyRouteTable" with the subnet "MySubnet" in the VNet "MyVNet" within the resource group "MyResourceGroup". By leveraging these features, users can create flexible and secure networking environments in Azure that meet their specific requirements and use cases. Whether deploying a simple web application or a complex multi-tiered architecture, VNets provide the foundation for building scalable, resilient, and highly available cloud-based solutions. With Azure CLI, users have the power and flexibility to automate the creation and management of VNets and associated resources, enabling them to deploy and manage networking infrastructures with ease and efficiency. Configuring Public and Private IP Addresses is a crucial aspect of setting up network connectivity for virtual machines (VMs), services, and resources in Azure. In Azure, public IP addresses are used to enable communication with resources over the internet, while private IP addresses are used for internal communication within a virtual network (VNet) or between VNets connected via virtual network peering or VPN gateways. To configure a public IP address for a resource in Azure, users can use the az network public-ip create command, specifying parameters such as resource group name and public IP address name. For example, the command az network public-ip create --resource-group MyResourceGroup --name MyPublicIP creates a public IP address named "MyPublicIP" in the resource group "MyResourceGroup". By default, Azure assigns dynamic public IP addresses, which are subject to change if the associated resource is deallocated and reallocated. To create a static public IP address that persists even when the associated resource is deallocated, users can add the --allocation-method Static parameter to the az network public-ip create command. For example, the command az network public-ip create --resource-group MyResourceGroup --name MyStaticPublicIP --allocation-method Static creates a static public IP address named "MyStaticPublicIP". Once created, users can associate the public IP address with a specific resource such as a virtual machine or load balancer using the az network public-ip update command. For example, the command az network public-ip update --resource-group MyResourceGroup --name MyPublicIP --allocation-method Static associates the public IP address "MyPublicIP" with the virtual machine or load balancer specified in the command. Private IP addresses, on the other hand, are used for internal communication within a VNet or between VNets connected via virtual network peering or VPN gateways. Azure automatically assigns private IP addresses to resources deployed within a VNet based on the address space specified for the VNet. To configure a private IP address for a resource, users simply need to deploy the resource within a subnet of the VNet and Azure will assign a private IP address from the subnet's address space. For example, when creating a virtual machine using the az vm create command, users can specify the subnet name as a parameter, and Azure will assign a private IP address to the virtual machine from the subnet's address space. Alternatively, users can manually assign a specific private IP address to a resource by configuring static IP address assignment within the resource's network settings. This can be done using the Azure portal, Azure PowerShell, or Azure CLI. For example, to configure a static private IP address for a virtual machine using Azure CLI, users can use the az network nic ip-config update command, specifying parameters such as resource group name, network interface card (NIC) name, and private IP address. For example, the command az network nic ip-config update --resource-group MyResourceGroup --nic-name MyNic --name *ipconfig1 --private-ip-address 10.0.0.5 updates the IP configuration named "ipconfig1" of the NIC "MyNic" in the resource group "MyResourceGroup" to use the static private IP address 10.0.0.5. By configuring public and private IP addresses effectively, users can establish secure and reliable network connectivity for their Azure resources, enabling seamless communication both within the virtual network and with external networks and services. Whether deploying virtual machines, load balancers, or other network resources, understanding how to configure IP addresses in Azure is essential for building scalable and resilient cloud-based infrastructures. With Azure CLI, users have the flexibility and power to automate the configuration of IP addresses and associated networking settings, enabling them to deploy and manage network resources with efficiency and ease.*

Chapter 4: Managing Virtual Networks with CLI

Managing Virtual Network Subnets in Azure is a critical aspect of designing and configuring network infrastructures to support various workloads and applications effectively. Subnets allow users to segment a virtual network (VNet) into smaller, more manageable units, enabling them to control network traffic flow, apply network security policies, and optimize resource placement. To create a subnet within a VNet using Azure CLI, users can utilize the az network vnet subnet create command, specifying parameters such as resource group name, VNet name, subnet name, and address prefix. For example, the command az network vnet subnet create --resource-group MyResourceGroup --vnet-name MyVNet --name MySubnet --address-prefixes 10.0.0.0/24 creates a subnet named "MySubnet" with the address prefix 10.0.0.0/24 within the VNet "MyVNet" in the resource group "MyResourceGroup". By creating multiple subnets within a VNet, users can logically group resources based on their function, application, or workload type, allowing for more granular control and management. Additionally, users can configure network security groups (NSGs) at the subnet level to enforce security policies and restrict traffic flow between subnets and external networks. NSGs act as a basic firewall, allowing users to define inbound and outbound security rules based on source and destination IP addresses, ports, and protocols. To associate an NSG with a subnet using Azure CLI, users can use the az network vnet subnet update command, specifying parameters such as resource group name, VNet name, subnet name, and NSG name. For example, the command az network vnet subnet update --resource-group MyResourceGroup --vnet-name MyVNet --name MySubnet --network-security-group MyNSG associates the NSG named "MyNSG" with the subnet "MySubnet" in the VNet "MyVNet" within the resource group "MyResourceGroup". This allows users to apply consistent security policies across all resources within the subnet, helping to protect against unauthorized access and malicious threats. In addition to NSGs, users can also configure route tables at the subnet level to control the flow of network traffic within the VNet and to external destinations. Route tables allow users to define routes that specify where traffic should be directed based on destination IP addresses. To associate a route table with a subnet using Azure CLI, users can use the az network vnet subnet update command, specifying parameters such as resource group name, VNet name, subnet name, and route table name. For example, the command az network vnet subnet update --resource-group MyResourceGroup --vnet-name MyVNet --name MySubnet --route-table MyRouteTable associates the route table named "MyRouteTable" with the subnet "MySubnet" in the VNet "MyVNet" within the resource group "MyResourceGroup". By leveraging these features, users can create flexible and secure networking environments in Azure that meet their specific requirements and use cases. Whether deploying web applications, databases, or virtual machines, managing virtual network subnets effectively is essential for optimizing performance, ensuring scalability, and maintaining security. With Azure CLI, users have the power and flexibility to automate the creation, configuration, and management of subnets and associated networking settings, enabling them to deploy and manage network resources with efficiency and ease. Implementing Network Security Groups (NSGs) with CLI commands is a fundamental aspect of securing network traffic within Azure virtual networks, providing granular control over inbound and outbound traffic to and from Azure resources. NSGs act as a basic firewall, allowing users to define rules that permit or deny traffic based on source and destination IP addresses, ports, and protocols. To create an NSG using Azure CLI, users can use the az network nsg create command, specifying parameters such as resource group name and NSG name. For example, the command az network nsg create --resource-group MyResourceGroup --name MyNSG creates an NSG named "MyNSG" in the resource group "MyResourceGroup". Once created, users can define inbound and outbound security rules for the NSG using the az network nsg rule create command. For *example, the command az network nsg rule create --resource-group MyResourceGroup --nsg-name MyNSG --name AllowSSH --protocol Tcp --direction Inbound --priority 100 --source-address-prefixes '*' --source-port-ranges '*' --destination-address-prefixes '*' --destination-port-ranges 22 --access Allow creates a security rule named "AllowSSH" that allows inbound SSH traffic (port 22) from any source to any destination. Users can also configure security rules to deny specific types of traffic, block access to certain IP addresses or port ranges, or restrict communication between resources within the same subnet. By associating an NSG with a subnet or network interface card (NIC) attached to a virtual machine, users can apply network security policies at the network level, ensuring consistent enforcement across all resources within the subnet or attached to the NIC. To associate an NSG with a subnet using Azure CLI, users can use the az network vnet subnet update command, specifying parameters such as resource group name, VNet name, subnet name, and NSG name. For example, the command az network vnet subnet update --resource-group MyResourceGroup --vnet-name MyVNet --name MySubnet --network-security-group MyNSG associates the NSG named "MyNSG" with the subnet "MySubnet" in the VNet "MyVNet" within the resource group "MyResourceGroup". Similarly, to associate an NSG with a NIC using Azure CLI, users can use the az network nic update command, specifying parameters such as resource* *group name, NIC name, and NSG name. For example, the command az network nic update --resource-group MyResourceGroup --name MyNic --network-security-group MyNSG associates the NSG named "MyNSG" with the NIC "MyNic" within the resource group "MyResourceGroup". By implementing NSGs with CLI commands, users can enforce network security policies effectively, protect against unauthorized access and malicious threats, and ensure the integrity and confidentiality of their Azure resources. Whether deploying virtual machines, load balancers, or other network resources, NSGs provide a flexible and scalable solution for securing network traffic within Azure virtual networks. With Azure CLI, users have the power and flexibility to automate the creation, configuration, and management of NSGs and associated security rules, enabling them to enforce security policies consistently across their Azure environments and protect their resources from potential security vulnerabilities and attacks.*

Chapter 5: Configuring Subnets and Network Security Groups

Configuring subnet-to-subnet communication is essential for establishing connectivity between different subnets within a virtual network (VNet) in Azure, enabling resources deployed in separate subnets to communicate with each other seamlessly. This configuration is particularly useful for building multi-tiered architectures, where different components of an application or service are deployed in separate subnets to achieve isolation, scalability, and security. In Azure, subnet-to-subnet communication can be achieved through various methods, including network virtual appliance (NVA), virtual network peering, and VPN gateway. One approach to enabling subnet-to-subnet communication is by deploying a network virtual appliance (NVA) within the virtual network. NVAs are virtual machines or appliances that provide advanced networking features such as routing, firewalling, and network address translation (NAT). To deploy an NVA in Azure, users can use the Azure portal or Azure CLI commands such as az vm create to create a virtual machine and az network nic create to create a network interface card (NIC) for the virtual machine. Once the NVA is deployed, users can configure routing tables and network security rules to route traffic between subnets and enforce security policies. Another method for enabling subnet-to-subnet communication is through virtual network peering, which allows users to connect two VNets together using a virtual network peering connection. To create a virtual network peering connection using Azure CLI, users can use the az network vnet peering create command, specifying parameters such as resource group name, VNet name, and peering name. For example, the command az network vnet peering create --resource-group MyResourceGroup --name MyPeering --vnet-name VNet1 --remote-vnet VNet2 --allow-vnet-access creates a virtual network peering connection named "MyPeering" between VNet1 and VNet2 within the resource group "MyResourceGroup". Once the peering connection is established, traffic can flow between the two VNets, allowing resources in one subnet to communicate with resources in the other subnet. Additionally, users can configure network security rules and route tables to control traffic flow and enforce security policies between the peered VNets. Alternatively, users can establish subnet-to-subnet communication using VPN gateway, which allows users to connect on-premises networks or VNets in different regions using a secure VPN connection. To create a VPN gateway in Azure, users can use the az network vnet-gateway create command, specifying parameters such as resource group name, VNet name, and gateway type. For example, the command az network vnet-gateway *create --resource-group MyResourceGroup --name MyVpnGateway --vnet MyVNet --gateway-type Vpn creates a VPN gateway named "MyVpnGateway" within the VNet "MyVNet" in the resource group "MyResourceGroup". Once the VPN gateway is created, users can configure site-to-site or VNet-to-VNet connections to establish VPN tunnels between different subnets or VNets. This allows resources in one subnet to communicate securely with resources in another subnet over the VPN connection. By configuring subnet-to-subnet communication in Azure, users can create flexible and scalable network architectures that meet their specific requirements and use cases. Whether deploying multi-tiered applications, connecting on-premises networks, or implementing disaster recovery solutions, subnet-to-subnet communication enables seamless connectivity between different components of the network, improving performance, reliability, and security. With Azure CLI, users have the flexibility and power to automate the configuration and management of subnet-to-subnet communication, enabling them to deploy and manage network resources with efficiency and ease.*

Enforcing network security policies is a crucial aspect of maintaining the integrity, confidentiality, and availability of data and resources within a network environment, whether on-premises or in the cloud. In Azure, network security policies can be enforced using various tools and techniques, including network *security groups (NSGs), Azure Firewall, and third-party security appliances. NSGs are a foundational component of Azure's network security model, providing a basic level of firewalling and traffic filtering at the network level. To create an NSG in Azure using the CLI, users can utilize the az network nsg create command, specifying parameters such as resource group name and NSG name. For example, az network nsg create --resource-group MyResourceGroup --name MyNSG creates an NSG named "MyNSG" in the resource group "MyResourceGroup". Once created, users can define inbound and outbound security rules for the NSG using the az network nsg rule create command. For instance, az network nsg rule create --resource-group MyResourceGroup --nsg-name MyNSG --name AllowSSH --protocol Tcp --direction Inbound --priority 100 --source-address-prefixes '*' --source-port-ranges '*' --destination-address-prefixes '*' --destination-port-ranges 22 --access Allow creates a security rule named "AllowSSH" that allows inbound SSH traffic (port 22) from any source to any destination. By associating an NSG with a subnet or network interface card (NIC) attached to a virtual machine, users can apply network security policies at the network level, ensuring consistent enforcement across all resources within the subnet or attached to the NIC. To associate an NSG with a subnet using Azure CLI, users can use the az network vnet subnet update command, specifying parameters such as resource group name,*

VNet name, subnet name, and NSG name. For example, az network vnet subnet update --resource-group MyResourceGroup --vnet-name MyVNet --name MySubnet --network-security-group MyNSG associates the NSG named "MyNSG" with the subnet "MySubnet" in the VNet "MyVNet" within the resource group "MyResourceGroup". Additionally, Azure Firewall is a managed, cloud-based firewall service that provides advanced threat protection and application-level filtering for Azure resources. To deploy Azure Firewall using the CLI, users can use the az network firewall create command, specifying parameters such as resource group name and firewall name. For example, az network firewall create --resource-group MyResourceGroup --name MyFirewall creates an Azure Firewall named "MyFirewall" in the resource group "MyResourceGroup". Once deployed, users can configure network rules and application rules to control inbound and outbound traffic to and from Azure resources, ensuring compliance with organizational security policies and regulatory requirements. Third-party security appliances can also be used to enforce network security policies in Azure, providing additional layers of protection and customization options. Users can deploy third-party security appliances as virtual machines or appliances within their Azure environment and configure them to inspect and filter network traffic according to their specific security requirements. By leveraging these tools and techniques, organizations can enforce *network security policies effectively, protect against unauthorized access and malicious threats, and ensure the confidentiality, integrity, and availability of their data and resources in Azure. Whether deploying virtual machines, web applications, or database services, enforcing network security policies is essential for mitigating security risks and maintaining a secure and compliant network environment. With Azure CLI, users have the flexibility and power to automate the deployment, configuration, and management of network security policies, enabling them to enforce consistent security controls across their Azure environment and protect their resources from potential security vulnerabilities and attacks.*

Chapter 6: Connecting Virtual Networks: Peering and Gateway Configuration

Establishing Virtual Network Peering Connections in Azure is a fundamental technique for enabling communication between virtual networks (VNets) within the same region or across regions, facilitating the creation of more complex and interconnected network topologies. Virtual network peering allows VNets to communicate with each other as if they were part of the same network, enabling seamless access to resources and services deployed across different VNets. To establish a virtual network peering connection using Azure CLI, users can utilize the az network vnet peering create command, specifying parameters such as resource group name, VNet name, and peering name. For example, the command az network vnet peering create --resource-group MyResourceGroup --name MyPeering --vnet-name VNet1 --remote-vnet VNet2 --allow-vnet-access creates a virtual network peering connection named "MyPeering" between VNet1 and VNet2 within the resource group "MyResourceGroup". Once the peering connection is established, traffic can flow between the two VNets, allowing resources in one VNet to communicate with resources in the other VNet seamlessly. Additionally, users can configure peering settings such as access permissions, traffic forwarding, and gateway transit to control the behavior of the peering connection and restrict access to specific resources or services. For example, users can use the --allow-vnet-access parameter to enable connectivity between VNets and the --allow-forwarded-traffic parameter to allow forwarded traffic from one VNet to another. Users can also enable gateway transit to allow traffic from a peered VNet to flow through a virtual network gateway deployed in another VNet. This is particularly useful for scenarios where users need to establish site-to-site or hybrid connectivity between on-premises networks and VNets in Azure. To enable gateway transit for a virtual network peering connection using Azure CLI, users can use the az network vnet peering update command, specifying parameters such as resource group name, VNet name, peering name, and gateway transit flag. For example, the command az network vnet peering update --resource-group MyResourceGroup --name MyPeering --vnet-name VNet1 --set allowGatewayTransit=true enables gateway transit for the peering connection named "MyPeering" in the VNet "VNet1" within the resource group "MyResourceGroup". Once gateway transit is enabled, traffic from the peered VNet can flow through the virtual network gateway deployed in the other VNet, allowing users to establish secure and reliable connectivity between on-premises networks and VNets in Azure. Furthermore, users can configure virtual network peering using Azure PowerShell or the

Azure portal, providing flexibility and choice in how they manage and configure their network resources. In addition to enabling connectivity between VNets within the same region, Azure also supports global virtual network peering, allowing users to establish peering connections between VNets deployed in different regions. This enables users to create global, interconnected network architectures that span multiple regions and provide seamless access to resources and services across geographical boundaries. By establishing virtual network peering connections in Azure, users can create flexible, scalable, and interconnected network architectures that meet their specific requirements and use cases. Whether deploying multi-tiered applications, implementing disaster recovery solutions, or enabling hybrid connectivity, virtual network peering provides a powerful mechanism for connecting VNets and facilitating communication between resources and services deployed across different network boundaries. With Azure CLI, users have the flexibility and power to automate the deployment, configuration, and management of virtual network peering connections, enabling them to establish secure, reliable, and interconnected network environments in Azure with ease and efficiency.

Configuring Virtual Network Gateways (VNGs) for connectivity is essential for establishing secure and reliable network connections between on-premises networks, virtual networks (VNets), and other Azure services, enabling seamless communication and data exchange across different network boundaries. In Azure, VNGs serve as the entry and exit points for network traffic flowing between on-premises networks and Azure VNets, providing features such as site-to-site VPN, point-to-site VPN, and ExpressRoute connectivity options. To configure a VNG in Azure using CLI commands, users can utilize the az network vnet-gateway create command, specifying parameters such as resource group name, VNet name, and gateway type. For instance, the command az network vnet-gateway create --resource-group MyResourceGroup --name MyVNG --vnet MyVNet --gateway-type Vpn creates a VNG named "MyVNG" within the VNet "MyVNet" in the resource group "MyResourceGroup" with VPN gateway type. Once the VNG is created, users can configure the specific connectivity options based on their requirements. For site-to-site VPN connectivity, users need to create a VPN gateway and a local network gateway (LNG) representing the on-premises network. To create an LNG in Azure, users can use the az network local-gateway create command, specifying parameters such as resource group name, LNG name, and IP address of the on-premises VPN device. For example, the command az network local-gateway create --resource-group MyResourceGroup --name MyLNG --gateway-ip-address 203.0.113.10 --local-address-prefixes 192.168.0.0/16 creates an LNG named

"MyLNG" in the resource group "MyResourceGroup" with the gateway IP address 203.0.113.10 and local address prefix 192.168.0.0/16. Once the LNG is created, users can associate it with the VNG using the az network vpn-gateway connection create command, specifying parameters such as resource group name, VNG name, connection name, and LNG name. For example, the command az network vpn-gateway connection create --resource-group MyResourceGroup --name MyConnection --gateway-name MyVNG --local-gateway2 MyLNG --shared-key Abc123 creates a VPN connection named "MyConnection" between the VNG "MyVNG" and the LNG "MyLNG" in the resource group "MyResourceGroup" with a shared key "Abc123". Once the VPN connection is established, traffic can flow securely between the on-premises network and Azure VNet over the VPN tunnel. For point-to-site VPN connectivity, users can configure VNGs to support VPN connections from individual client devices, such as laptops or mobile devices, using certificates or authentication keys. To enable point-to-site VPN connectivity for a VNG, users can use the az network vnet-gateway vpn-client generate command to generate VPN client configuration files and certificates, which can then be distributed to individual client devices for connection setup. For ExpressRoute connectivity, users need to provision an ExpressRoute circuit and configure the VNG to establish connectivity with the ExpressRoute circuit. To create an ExpressRoute circuit in Azure, users can *use the Azure portal or CLI commands such as az network express-route create. Once the ExpressRoute circuit is provisioned, users can associate it with the VNG using the az network vnet-gateway update command, specifying parameters such as resource group name, VNG name, and ExpressRoute circuit ID. For example, the command az network vnet-gateway update --resource-group MyResourceGroup --name MyVNG   --set expressRoute.gateway1.id="/subscriptions/{subscripti onId}/resourceGroups/{resourceGroupName}/provider s/Microsoft.Network/expressRouteCircuits/{circuitNa me}" associates the VNG "MyVNG" with the ExpressRoute circuit specified by the circuit ID. Once the association is established, traffic can flow between the on-premises network and Azure VNet over the ExpressRoute circuit, providing high-speed, low-latency connectivity with guaranteed bandwidth and reliability. By configuring VNGs for connectivity in Azure, users can establish secure and reliable network connections between on-premises networks, VNets, and other Azure services, enabling seamless communication and data exchange across different network boundaries. Whether deploying site-to-site VPN, point-to-site VPN, or ExpressRoute connectivity options, VNGs provide a flexible and scalable solution for connecting on-premises networks with Azure resources and services. With Azure CLI, users have the flexibility and power to automate the deployment, configuration, and management of VNGs and associated connectivity options, enabling them to establish secure, reliable, and interconnected network environments in Azure with ease and efficiency.*

Chapter 7: Implementing Network Monitoring and Diagnostics

Setting up network monitoring alerts in Azure is crucial for proactively identifying and mitigating potential issues or anomalies in network performance and availability, ensuring the reliability and stability of network infrastructures. Azure provides a comprehensive set of monitoring and alerting tools, including Azure Monitor and Azure Security Center, which enable users to monitor network traffic, performance metrics, and security events in real-time and trigger alerts based on predefined conditions. To set up network monitoring alerts using Azure Monitor, users can utilize the az monitor metrics alert create command, specifying parameters such as resource group name, alert name, resource type, metric name, and threshold values. For instance, the command az monitor metrics alert create --resource-group MyResourceGroup --name HighNetworkTraffic --resource /subscriptions/{subscriptionId}/resourceGroups/{resourceGroupName}/providers/Microsoft.Network/networkInterfaces/{nicName} --metric "BytesTransmitted" --operator GreaterThan --threshold 1000000 --evaluation-frequency 5 --

window-size 15 --description "Alert triggered when network traffic exceeds 1 MB per 5 minutes" creates a network monitoring alert named "HighNetworkTraffic" in the resource group "MyResourceGroup" for the network interface specified by the NIC name, triggering an alert when the transmitted bytes exceed 1 MB per 5 minutes. Additionally, users can configure alert rules to send notifications via email, SMS, webhook, or Azure Functions when an alert condition is met, allowing for timely response and resolution of network issues. For example, users can use the --action parameter to specify the action group associated with the alert rule, which contains the notification settings and action to be taken when the alert fires. Users can create an action group using the az monitor action-group create command, specifying parameters such as action group name, short name, and notification settings. For instance, the command az monitor action-group create --name MyActionGroup --short-name MyActionGroup --email test@example.com --sms +1234567890 creates an action group named "MyActionGroup" with email and SMS notifications enabled for the specified email address and phone number. Once the action group is created, users can associate it with the alert rule using the --action parameter, ensuring that notifications are sent to the designated recipients when the alert condition is met. In addition to Azure Monitor, users can leverage Azure Security Center to set up network security alerts and monitor for potential security threats or vulnerabilities in network configurations. Azure Security Center provides built-in security policies and recommendations for network security best practices, allowing users to detect and remediate security issues proactively. To set up network security alerts using Azure Security Center, users can utilize the az security alert command, specifying parameters such as alert name, resource group name, and security policy. For example, the command az security alert create --name MySecurityAlert --resource-group MyResourceGroup --policy "/subscriptions/{subscriptionId}/providers/Microsoft .Security/policies/{policyName}" creates a network security alert named "MySecurityAlert" in the resource group "MyResourceGroup" based on the specified security policy. Once the alert is created, users can configure notification settings and remediation actions to be taken when a security threat is detected, helping to protect network resources from potential attacks or breaches. By setting up network monitoring alerts in Azure, users can proactively monitor network performance, detect security threats, and respond to critical events in real-time, ensuring the reliability, security, and availability of network infrastructures. Whether monitoring for high network traffic, network security vulnerabilities, or performance anomalies, Azure provides a robust set of monitoring and alerting tools that enable users to stay informed and take action to mitigate potential risks and maintain network integrity. With Azure CLI, users have the flexibility and power to automate the deployment, configuration, and management of network monitoring alerts, enabling them to establish proactive monitoring practices and effectively manage network resources in Azure. Utilizing Azure Diagnostics for troubleshooting is an essential aspect of maintaining the performance, reliability, and security of Azure resources and applications, providing insights into the health and behavior of Azure services and infrastructure components. Azure Diagnostics allows users to collect and analyze diagnostic data, logs, and metrics from various Azure resources, including virtual machines, web apps, and storage accounts, enabling them to identify and resolve issues quickly and effectively. To enable Azure Diagnostics for a virtual machine using Azure CLI, users can utilize the az vm diagnostics set command, specifying parameters such as resource group name, virtual machine name, and diagnostics settings. For example, the command az vm diagnostics set --resource-group MyResourceGroup --vm-name MyVM --settings "DiagnosticsMonitorConfiguration": {

"eventVolume": "Medium" } --protected-settings "{\"storageAccountName\": \"mystorageaccount\", \"storageAccountKey\": \"mykey\" }" configures Azure Diagnostics for the virtual machine "MyVM" in the resource group "MyResourceGroup" to collect medium-level diagnostic events and store them in the specified storage account with the provided access key. Once Azure Diagnostics is enabled for the virtual machine, users can monitor and analyze diagnostic data using Azure Monitor, Azure Log Analytics, or other monitoring and analytics tools, allowing them to gain insights into the performance, availability, and security of the virtual machine and troubleshoot issues as they arise. In addition to virtual machines, users can also enable Azure Diagnostics for other Azure resources, such as Azure App Service web apps, using Azure CLI commands specific to each resource type. For instance, to enable diagnostics logging for an Azure App Service web app, users can use the az webapp log config command, specifying parameters such as resource group name, web app name, and log level. For example, the command az webapp log config --resource-group MyResourceGroup --name MyWebApp --application-logging true --detailed-error-messages true --failed-request-tracing true enables application logging, detailed error messages, and failed request tracing for the web app "MyWebApp" in the resource group

"MyResourceGroup". Once enabled, diagnostic logs are generated and stored in the configured storage account or Log Analytics workspace, allowing users to analyze web app performance and troubleshoot issues effectively. Furthermore, users can leverage Azure Monitor to create custom diagnostic logs and metrics queries, dashboards, and alerts based on specific performance indicators or events, enabling them to monitor Azure resources proactively and detect and respond to issues in real-time. For example, users can use the Azure Monitor Metrics Explorer to visualize and analyze performance metrics such as CPU usage, memory utilization, and network throughput for virtual machines, enabling them to identify performance bottlenecks and optimize resource usage accordingly. By utilizing Azure Diagnostics for troubleshooting, users can gain valuable insights into the health and performance of Azure resources and applications, enabling them to identify and resolve issues quickly and effectively. Whether troubleshooting performance issues, analyzing application logs, or detecting security threats, Azure Diagnostics provides a comprehensive set of tools and capabilities that empower users to maintain the reliability, availability, and security of their Azure environment. With Azure CLI, users have the flexibility and power to automate the deployment, configuration, and management of Azure

Diagnostics settings for various Azure resources, enabling them to establish proactive monitoring practices and effectively troubleshoot issues as they arise.

Chapter 8: Securing Your Azure Network Resources

Implementing Role-Based Access Control (RBAC) for network security is a fundamental aspect of managing access to Azure resources and ensuring the confidentiality, integrity, and availability of data and services within a network environment. RBAC enables users to control who has access to Azure resources and what actions they can perform, allowing organizations to enforce security policies and comply with regulatory requirements effectively. In Azure, RBAC is based on predefined roles that encompass a set of permissions required to perform specific tasks or operations on Azure resources. To implement RBAC for network security using Azure CLI, users can utilize commands such as az role assignment create to assign roles to users, groups, or service principals, specifying parameters such as role name, resource group name, and scope. For example, the command az role assignment create --assignee john.doe@example.com --role "Network Contributor" --scope "/subscriptions/{subscriptionId}/resourceGroups/{resourceGroupName}" assigns the "Network Contributor" role to the user "john.doe@example.com" at the specified scope. Once the role assignment is created, the user gains the permissions associated with the role, allowing them to manage network resources within the specified scope. Additionally, users can create custom RBAC roles to tailor permissions according to their specific security requirements using the *az role definition create* command. For instance, the command *az role definition create --role-definition "path/to/role-definition.json"* creates a custom RBAC role based on the JSON file containing the role definition. Users can specify the permissions, actions, and scope for the custom role to meet their organization's security policies and compliance needs. By implementing RBAC for network security, organizations can enforce the principle of least privilege, granting users only the permissions necessary to perform their job responsibilities and reducing the risk of unauthorized access or data breaches. RBAC also enables organizations to segregate duties and responsibilities effectively, ensuring that sensitive network resources are accessed and managed only by authorized personnel. Furthermore, RBAC integrates seamlessly with Azure Active Directory (AD), allowing organizations to leverage existing user identities, groups, and access policies for authentication and authorization purposes. Users can use Azure AD groups to manage access to Azure resources at scale, simplifying the management of access permissions and ensuring consistency across the organization. To assign roles to Azure AD groups using Azure CLI, users can use commands such as *az role assignment create* with the *--assignee* parameter set to the group's object ID. For example, the command *az role assignment create --*

assignee "{groupObjectId}" --role "Network Contributor" --scope "/subscriptions/{subscriptionId}/resourceGroups/{resourceGroupName}" assigns the "Network Contributor" role to the Azure AD group specified by its object ID at the specified scope. Once the role assignment is created, all members of the Azure AD group inherit the permissions associated with the role, allowing them to manage network resources within the specified scope. In addition to managing access permissions, RBAC enables organizations to audit and monitor user activity effectively, allowing them to track changes to network resources, detect security incidents, and investigate suspicious behavior. Azure Monitor logs provide detailed information about role assignments, resource modifications, and access attempts, enabling organizations to generate reports, analyze trends, and enforce compliance with security policies and regulatory requirements. By leveraging RBAC for network security, organizations can strengthen their security posture, mitigate the risk of unauthorized access or data breaches, and maintain the confidentiality, integrity, and availability of their network resources in Azure. With Azure CLI, users have the flexibility and power to automate the deployment, configuration, and management of RBAC roles and assignments, enabling them to establish robust access control policies and enforce security best practices effectively. Encrypting data in transit with Azure Networking is a *critical aspect of ensuring the security and privacy of data as it travels between network endpoints within Azure and between Azure and external networks. Azure provides several mechanisms for encrypting data in transit, including Transport Layer Security (TLS) for secure communication over the internet, Virtual Network (VNet) peering for encrypted communication between Azure VNets, and Virtual Private Network (VPN) and ExpressRoute for secure connectivity between on-premises networks and Azure VNets. To enable TLS encryption for web applications hosted in Azure App Service, users can configure SSL/TLS certificates for custom domains using the Azure CLI. The command az webapp config ssl bind allows users to bind an SSL certificate to an Azure App Service web app, specifying parameters such as resource group name, web app name, and SSL certificate details. For example, the command az webapp config ssl bind --resource-group MyResourceGroup --name MyWebApp --certificate-thumbprint {thumbprint} --ssl-type SNI binds an SSL certificate with the specified thumbprint to the web app "MyWebApp" in the resource group "MyResourceGroup" using Server Name Indication (SNI) for SSL termination. Once the SSL certificate is bound, the web app uses TLS encryption to secure communication between clients and the web server, protecting sensitive data such as login credentials and personal information from eavesdropping and tampering. Additionally, users can enable TLS* encryption for Azure SQL Database to encrypt data transmitted between client applications and the database server using SSL/TLS. To enforce SSL/TLS encryption for Azure SQL Database connections, users can configure the "Enforce SSL connection" setting using the Azure portal or Azure CLI. The command az sql server update --resource-group MyResourceGroup --name myserver --ssl-enforcement Enabled enables SSL/TLS encryption enforcement for the SQL server "myserver" in the resource group "MyResourceGroup", ensuring that all client connections to the database server are encrypted using SSL/TLS. By encrypting data in transit with TLS, organizations can protect sensitive information from unauthorized access and interception while ensuring compliance with data protection regulations and industry standards. In addition to TLS encryption, Azure VNets support encrypted communication between virtual machines (VMs) and other network endpoints within the VNet using VNet peering. VNet peering establishes a private, encrypted connection between VNets, allowing VMs in different VNets to communicate securely without exposing traffic to the public internet. To create a VNet peering connection between two VNets using Azure CLI, users can use the az network vnet peering create command, specifying parameters such as resource group name, VNet name, and peering settings. For example, the command az network vnet peering create --name MyPeering --resource-group MyResourceGroup --vnet-name VNet1

--remote-vnet VNet2 --allow-vnet-access creates a peering connection named "MyPeering" between VNet1 and VNet2 in the resource group "MyResourceGroup", allowing traffic to flow securely between the two VNets. Once the VNet peering connection is established, data transmitted between VMs in the peered VNets is encrypted using Azure's built-in encryption mechanisms, ensuring the confidentiality and integrity of the transmitted data. Furthermore, organizations can establish secure connectivity between on-premises networks and Azure VNets using VPN or ExpressRoute. VPN enables encrypted communication between on-premises networks and Azure VNets over the public internet, while ExpressRoute provides private, dedicated connections over a secure, high-speed network link. To configure VPN or ExpressRoute for secure connectivity with Azure VNets using Azure CLI, users can use commands such as az network vpn-gateway create for VPN gateway deployment or az network express-route circuit create for ExpressRoute circuit provisioning, specifying parameters such as resource group name, gateway type, and connection settings. Once the VPN gateway or ExpressRoute circuit is provisioned, users can establish encrypted connections between on-premises networks and Azure VNets, ensuring secure data transmission and compliance with security policies and regulatory requirements. By encrypting data in transit with Azure Networking, organizations can protect sensitive information from unauthorized *access and interception while ensuring the integrity and confidentiality of data transmitted over Azure networks. Whether securing web applications, database connections, or inter-VNet communication, Azure provides a range of encryption options and tools that enable organizations to implement robust security controls and mitigate the risk of data breaches and cyber attacks. With Azure CLI, users have the flexibility and power to automate the deployment, configuration, and management of encryption settings for Azure Networking resources, enabling them to establish secure, compliant, and resilient network architectures with ease and efficiency.*

Chapter 9: Integrating Azure Networking with Other Azure Services

Integrating virtual networks with Azure virtual machines (VMs) is a crucial step in establishing secure, scalable, and interconnected network architectures within the Azure cloud environment, enabling seamless communication between VMs, applications, and services while maintaining isolation and security boundaries. Azure virtual networks (VNets) provide a private and isolated network environment for Azure resources, allowing users to define IP address ranges, subnets, and network security groups to control traffic flow and enforce security policies. To integrate Azure VNets with virtual machines, users can deploy VMs within the desired VNet and subnet using the Azure CLI. The command az vm create allows users to create a virtual machine in a specified resource group, VNet, and subnet, specifying parameters such as VM name, image, size, and networking configuration. For example, the command az vm create --resource-group MyResourceGroup --name MyVM --image UbuntuLTS --vnet-name MyVNet --subnet MySubnet --public-ip-address "" creates a virtual machine named "MyVM" in the resource group "MyResourceGroup", within the VNet "MyVNet" and subnet "MySubnet", without a public IP address. Once the VM is deployed within the VNet, it becomes part of the VNet's address space and can communicate with other resources and services within the same VNet. Additionally, users can configure network security groups (NSGs) to control inbound and outbound traffic to and from VMs within the VNet. NSGs allow users to define security rules that specify allowed or denied traffic based on source IP address, destination IP address, port, and protocol. To create an NSG rule using Azure CLI, users can utilize the az network nsg rule create command, specifying parameters such as resource group name, NSG name, rule name, and rule properties. For example, the command az network nsg rule create --resource-group MyResourceGroup --nsg-name MyNSG --name AllowHTTP --priority 100 --source-address-prefixes '*' --source-port-ranges '*' --destination-address-prefixes '*' --destination-port-ranges 80 --access Allow --protocol Tcp creates a network security group rule named "AllowHTTP" in the NSG "MyNSG" within the resource group "MyResourceGroup", allowing inbound traffic on port 80 (HTTP) from any source IP address. By associating the NSG with the subnet containing the VMs, users can enforce network security policies and restrict unauthorized access to VMs and applications. Furthermore, users can establish network connectivity between Azure VNets and on-premises networks or other Azure VNets using virtual network peering or VPN gateway connections. Virtual network peering enables users to connect VNets within the same region or across different regions, allowing VMs and resources in peered VNets to communicate securely and efficiently. To create a VNet peering connection using Azure CLI, users can utilize the az network vnet peering create command, specifying parameters such as resource group name, VNet name, peering name, and peering properties. For example, the command az network vnet peering create --resource-group MyResourceGroup --name MyPeering --vnet-name VNet1 --remote-vnet VNet2 --allow-vnet-access creates a VNet peering connection named "MyPeering" between VNet1 and VNet2 in the resource group "MyResourceGroup", allowing traffic to flow securely between the two VNets. Alternatively, users can establish VPN gateway connections between Azure VNets and on-premises networks using Azure VPN gateways. VPN gateways provide secure, encrypted connections over the public internet, allowing VMs and resources in Azure VNets to communicate with on-premises networks as if they were connected directly. To create a VPN gateway connection using Azure CLI, users can use the az network vpn-connection create command, specifying parameters such as resource group name, gateway name, connection name, and connection properties. For example, the command *az network vpn-connection create --resource-group MyResourceGroup --name MyConnection --vnet-gateway1 MyVNG --local-gateway2 MyLNG --shared-key Abc123* creates a VPN connection named "MyConnection" between the VPN gateway "MyVNG" and the local network gateway "MyLNG" in the resource group "MyResourceGroup", with a shared key "Abc123" for authentication. Once the VPN connection is established, traffic can flow securely between Azure VNets and on-premises networks, enabling seamless integration and communication between cloud and on-premises resources. By integrating virtual networks with Azure virtual machines, users can build flexible, scalable, and secure network architectures that meet their business requirements and enable efficient communication and collaboration between cloud and on-premises environments. With Azure CLI, users have the flexibility and power to deploy, configure, and manage virtual machines, virtual networks, and network security settings, enabling them to establish robust and reliable network infrastructures in Azure with ease and efficiency. Leveraging Azure Networking for storage solutions is a crucial aspect of building scalable, reliable, and high-performance cloud storage architectures that meet the evolving needs of modern applications and workloads. Azure Networking provides a range of services and features that enable seamless integration with Azure Storage, allowing users to optimize data transfer, ensure data security, and maximize storage performance across distributed environments. One of the key components of Azure Networking for storage solutions is Azure Virtual Network (VNet), which enables users to create private and isolated network environments for Azure resources, including Azure Storage accounts. By deploying Azure Storage accounts within VNets, users can restrict access to storage resources, control network traffic, and enhance security by enforcing network-level policies and restrictions. To deploy an Azure Storage account within a VNet using Azure CLI, users can utilize the az storage account create command, specifying parameters such as resource group name, storage account name, location, and network settings. For example, the command az storage account create --name mystorageaccount --resource-group MyResourceGroup --location eastus --vnet-name MyVNet --subnet MySubnet creates a storage account named "mystorageaccount" in the resource group "MyResourceGroup", located in the "East US" region, and associated with the VNet "MyVNet" and subnet "MySubnet". Once the storage account is deployed within the VNet, all communication between the storage account and other resources within the same VNet occurs over the private network, reducing exposure to potential security threats and improving network performance. Additionally, users can leverage Azure Virtual Network service endpoints to optimize network traffic between Azure Storage accounts and resources within VNets, reducing latency and improving data transfer speeds. Azure Storage service endpoints enable users to access Azure Storage accounts over a private endpoint within the VNet, bypassing the public internet and reducing exposure to external threats. To create a service endpoint for an Azure Storage account using Azure CLI, users can use the az network vnet subnet update command, specifying parameters such as resource group name, VNet name, subnet name, and service endpoint type. For example, the command az network vnet subnet update --name MySubnet --resource-group MyResourceGroup --vnet-name MyVNet --service-endpoints Microsoft.Storage updates the subnet "MySubnet" within the VNet "MyVNet" in the resource group "MyResourceGroup" to enable the Microsoft.Storage service endpoint. Once the service endpoint is enabled, resources within the VNet can access the Azure Storage account over the private endpoint, ensuring secure and efficient data transfer between storage resources and applications. Furthermore, users can enhance data security and compliance by implementing network security controls such as network security groups (NSGs) and Azure Firewall to restrict access to Azure Storage resources based on network-level policies and rules. NSGs allow users to define inbound and outbound traffic rules for resources within VNets, while Azure Firewall provides centralized, stateful network security for VNets, allowing users to create and enforce application and network-level policies for traffic filtering and threat prevention. To create an NSG rule for an Azure Storage account using Azure CLI, users can utilize the az network nsg rule create command, specifying parameters such as resource group name, NSG name, rule name, and rule properties. For example, the command az network nsg rule create --resource-group MyResourceGroup --nsg-name MyNSG --name AllowStorageAccess --priority 100 --source-address-prefixes '*' --destination-port-ranges 443 --access Allow --protocol Tcp creates a network security group rule named "AllowStorageAccess" in the NSG "MyNSG" within the resource group "MyResourceGroup", allowing inbound traffic on port 443 (HTTPS) from any source IP address to the Azure Storage account. Once the NSG rule is applied, access to the storage account is restricted to authorized traffic based on the defined rules, ensuring data security and compliance with regulatory requirements. In summary, leveraging Azure Networking for storage solutions enables users to build secure, scalable, and *high-performance storage architectures that meet the demands of modern applications and workloads. By deploying Azure Storage accounts within VNets, optimizing network traffic with service endpoints, and implementing network security controls such as NSGs and Azure Firewall, users can ensure data security, enhance network performance, and comply with regulatory requirements while maximizing the value of their cloud storage investments. With Azure CLI, users have the flexibility and power to deploy, configure, and manage Azure Networking resources for storage solutions efficiently and effectively, enabling them to build resilient and reliable storage infrastructures in the Azure cloud.*

Chapter 10: Troubleshooting Common Networking Issues

Diagnosing connectivity issues with network monitoring tools is a critical aspect of maintaining the performance, reliability, and security of network infrastructures, allowing organizations to identify and resolve network problems quickly and effectively. Azure provides a range of network monitoring tools and services that enable users to monitor, analyze, and troubleshoot network connectivity issues across Azure resources, virtual networks, and hybrid environments. One of the key network monitoring tools offered by Azure is Azure Network Watcher, a service that provides network diagnostic and visualization capabilities for Azure resources, enabling users to identify and diagnose connectivity issues, performance bottlenecks, and security vulnerabilities. To diagnose connectivity issues with Azure Network Watcher using Azure CLI, users can utilize commands such as az network watcher test-connectivity, which allows users to test network connectivity between two virtual machines or endpoints within Azure VNets. For example, the command az network watcher test-connectivity --source-resource MyVM1 --destination-address 10.0.0.4 --dest-port 80 --direction outbound tests outbound connectivity from the virtual machine "MyVM1" to the IP address "10.0.0.4" on port 80, providing detailed information about the test results, including connectivity status, latency, and packet loss. Additionally, users can use Azure Network Watcher to capture network traffic and analyze packet data for troubleshooting purposes. The command az network watcher packet-capture create allows users to create packet capture sessions for monitoring network traffic on Azure VMs or subnets, specifying parameters such as resource group name, VM name, subnet name, and capture duration. For example, the command az network watcher packet-capture create --resource-group MyResourceGroup --vm MyVM --name MyPacketCapture --storage-account MyStorageAccount --duration 300 creates a packet capture session named "MyPacketCapture" on the virtual machine "MyVM" in the resource group "MyResourceGroup", storing the captured packet data in the storage account "MyStorageAccount" for a duration of 300 seconds. Once the packet capture session is created, users can analyze the captured data using network analysis tools or packet inspection software to identify network issues, anomalies, or security threats. Furthermore, Azure Network Watcher provides network topology visualization capabilities that allow users to visualize the connectivity and dependencies between Azure resources and VNets, helping users understand the network architecture and troubleshoot connectivity issues more effectively. The command az network watcher topology show retrieves the network topology information for a specified resource group or subscription, displaying the connectivity between Azure resources, VNets, and subnets in a graphical format. For example, the command az network watcher topology show --resource-group MyResourceGroup retrieves the network topology information for the resource group "MyResourceGroup", displaying the connectivity between resources and VNets in a visual diagram, including virtual machines, subnets, network security groups, and virtual network gateways. By visualizing the network topology, users can identify potential connectivity issues, misconfigurations, or bottlenecks and take corrective actions to resolve them proactively. In addition to Azure Network Watcher, Azure Monitor provides comprehensive network monitoring and logging capabilities that enable users to monitor and analyze network performance, traffic patterns, and security events across Azure resources and services. Azure Monitor collects telemetry data from various sources, including Azure network interfaces, virtual machines, and application gateways, allowing users to create custom metrics, alerts, and dashboards for monitoring network health and performance. The command az monitor metrics list retrieves the available metrics for a specified resource type and namespace, enabling users to monitor network performance metrics such as network traffic, latency, and packet loss. For example, the command az monitor metrics list --resource MyVM --resource-type Microsoft.Compute/virtualMachines --namespace 'Microsoft.Network' retrieves the available network metrics for the virtual machine "MyVM", allowing users to monitor network performance and detect anomalies or performance degradation. Additionally, users can use Azure Monitor logs to collect and analyze network-related logs and events for troubleshooting and forensic analysis. The command az monitor log-analytics query allows users to query log data stored in Azure Monitor logs using Azure Log Analytics Query Language (KQL), enabling users to search, filter, and analyze network-related logs for specific events or patterns. For example, the command az monitor log-analytics query --workspace MyWorkspace --query "Heartbeat | where ResourceId contains 'MyVM' | project TimeGenerated, Computer, ResourceId" retrieves the heartbeat logs for the virtual machine "MyVM" from the Azure Monitor workspace "MyWorkspace", displaying the timestamp, computer name, and resource ID for each heartbeat event. By leveraging Azure Monitor for network monitoring and logging, users can gain *visibility into network performance, troubleshoot connectivity issues, and ensure the reliability and security of their Azure network infrastructure. With Azure CLI, users have the flexibility and power to deploy, configure, and manage network monitoring tools and services for diagnosing connectivity issues effectively and efficiently, enabling them to maintain optimal network performance and reliability in Azure environments. Resolving DNS and IP addressing problems is a critical aspect of maintaining the availability, performance, and security of network infrastructures, ensuring that users can access resources and services reliably and efficiently. DNS (Domain Name System) is a fundamental protocol used to translate human-readable domain names into IP addresses, allowing users to access websites, applications, and services using familiar domain names rather than numerical IP addresses. When DNS resolution fails or returns incorrect IP addresses, users may experience connectivity issues, slow response times, or inability to access desired resources. Azure provides several tools and services to diagnose and resolve DNS and IP addressing problems, enabling users to troubleshoot and resolve issues quickly and effectively. One of the key tools for diagnosing DNS issues in Azure is Azure DNS, a scalable and reliable DNS hosting service that provides domain name resolution for Azure* services and resources. Users can use Azure DNS to host domain names and map them to IP addresses of Azure resources, enabling seamless access to web applications, virtual machines, and other Azure services. To resolve DNS issues with Azure DNS using Azure CLI, users can utilize commands such as az network dns record-set a list, which retrieves the list of DNS A records for a specified DNS zone, allowing users to verify the IP addresses associated with domain names. For example, the command az network dns record-set a list --zone-name mydomain.com --resource-group MyResourceGroup retrieves the list of A records for the DNS zone "mydomain.com" in the resource group "MyResourceGroup", displaying the IP addresses associated with each domain name. Additionally, users can use Azure CLI to create, update, or delete DNS records in Azure DNS zones, enabling them to manage DNS configurations and resolve DNS issues proactively. The command az network dns record-set a add-record allows users to add a new A record to a specified DNS zone, specifying parameters such as zone name, record set name, and IP address. For example, the command az network dns record-set a add-record --zone-name mydomain.com --resource-group MyResourceGroup --record-set-name www --ipv4-address 10.0.0.1 adds a new A record for the domain name "www.mydomain.com" in the DNS zone "mydomain.com", mapping it to the IP address

"10.0.0.1". By managing DNS records with Azure CLI, users can ensure accurate DNS resolution and prevent DNS-related connectivity issues. In addition to Azure DNS, users can leverage Azure Network Watcher to diagnose and troubleshoot DNS resolution problems within Azure virtual networks. Azure Network Watcher provides network diagnostic and visualization capabilities, allowing users to monitor, analyze, and troubleshoot network connectivity and performance issues. The command az network watcher troubleshoot --resource myvm --resource-type vm --destination 8.8.8.8 --direction from-resource allows users to troubleshoot DNS resolution issues from a specified virtual machine (VM) to a destination IP address, providing detailed diagnostic information about DNS resolution, network connectivity, and potential issues encountered. By analyzing the troubleshooting results, users can identify and resolve DNS-related problems, such as misconfigured DNS settings, DNS server unavailability, or DNS name resolution failures. Furthermore, users can use Azure CLI to diagnose and resolve IP addressing problems, such as IP address conflicts, subnet overlaps, or incorrect IP configurations. The command az network vnet list retrieves the list of virtual networks (VNets) in a specified resource group, allowing users to view the IP address ranges and subnet configurations of each VNet. For example, the command az network vnet

list --resource-group MyResourceGroup retrieves the list of VNets in the resource group "MyResourceGroup", displaying the IP address ranges and subnet configurations for each VNet. By reviewing VNet configurations with Azure CLI, users can identify potential IP addressing problems, such as overlapping IP address ranges or misconfigured subnets, and take corrective actions to resolve them. Additionally, users can use Azure CLI to update or modify IP address configurations for Azure resources, such as virtual machines, network interfaces, or load balancers, enabling them to resolve IP addressing conflicts or adjust IP configurations as needed. The command az network nic ip-config update allows users to update the IP configuration of a network interface (NIC) attached to a virtual machine, specifying parameters such as NIC name, resource group name, and new IP address settings. For example, the command az network nic ip-config update --name ipconfig1 --nic-name MyNic --resource-group MyResourceGroup --private-ip-address 10.0.0.5 --subnet MySubnet updates the IP configuration of the NIC "MyNic" in the resource group "MyResourceGroup", assigning the new IP address "10.0.0.5" to the NIC within the subnet "MySubnet". By updating IP configurations with Azure CLI, users can resolve IP addressing problems and ensure proper network connectivity for Azure resources. In summary, resolving DNS and

IP addressing problems is essential for maintaining the availability, performance, and security of network infrastructures in Azure environments. With Azure CLI, users have the flexibility and power to diagnose, troubleshoot, and resolve DNS and IP addressing issues effectively and efficiently, enabling them to ensure accurate DNS resolution, prevent IP addressing conflicts, and maintain optimal network connectivity for Azure resources and services.

BOOK 2
MASTERING AZURE CLI
INTERMEDIATE TECHNIQUES FOR NETWORKING IN THE CLOUD

ROB BOTWRIGHT

Chapter 1: Exploring Advanced Azure CLI Commands

Mastering CLI command structures is essential for efficiently navigating and utilizing command-line interfaces to manage and configure various systems, applications, and services. CLI (Command-Line Interface) commands are text-based instructions used to interact with computer programs and operating systems, enabling users to perform a wide range of tasks and operations without the need for graphical user interfaces. Understanding and mastering CLI command structures allow users to leverage the full power and flexibility of command-line interfaces, enabling them to perform complex operations quickly and accurately. One of the fundamental aspects of mastering CLI command structures is understanding the syntax and structure of CLI commands, including command names, options, arguments, and syntax conventions. CLI commands typically consist of a command name followed by optional options or arguments that modify the behavior of the command. For example, the command ls -l lists the contents of a directory in long format, with detailed information about each file or directory, where ls is the command name and -l is an option that specifies the long format. Similarly, understanding the syntax conventions used in CLI commands, such as the use of dashes or double dashes to denote options, square brackets to denote optional parameters, and angle brackets to denote required parameters, is essential for accurately constructing and executing CLI commands. For example, the command git commit -m "Initial commit" uses the -m option to specify a commit message, where the message "Initial commit" is provided as an argument to the -m option. Additionally, mastering CLI command structures involves understanding common command patterns and techniques used to compose and execute complex command sequences or pipelines. Command pipelines allow users to chain multiple commands together, passing the output of one command as input to the next command in the pipeline, enabling users to perform complex data processing or manipulation tasks efficiently. For example, the command cat file.txt | grep "pattern" reads the contents of a file named "file.txt" and passes it to the grep command, which filters the lines containing the specified pattern. By mastering command pipelines and techniques, users can streamline their workflows and perform complex tasks with ease. Furthermore, mastering CLI command structures involves familiarizing oneself with the available commands, options, and arguments supported by the target CLI environment, such as operating systems, programming languages, or cloud platforms. Many CLI environments provide built-in help systems or documentation that users can use to explore available commands and their usage syntax. For example, the command man ls displays the *manual page for the ls command in Unix-like operating systems, providing detailed information about the command's usage, options, and arguments. Similarly, cloud platforms such as Azure provide extensive documentation and resources for learning and mastering CLI commands for managing cloud resources and services. For example, the Azure CLI documentation provides detailed guides, tutorials, and examples for using CLI commands to deploy, configure, and manage Azure resources such as virtual machines, storage accounts, and databases. By leveraging documentation and resources provided by CLI environments, users can accelerate their learning and mastery of CLI command structures. Moreover, mastering CLI command structures involves practicing and experimenting with CLI commands in a sandbox or test environment, allowing users to gain hands-on experience and confidence in using CLI commands effectively. Hands-on practice enables users to explore different command options, experiment with command sequences, and troubleshoot common errors or issues that may arise when executing CLI commands. Additionally, users can leverage online forums, communities, and tutorials to learn from others, share knowledge, and troubleshoot problems collaboratively. By actively engaging with CLI communities and resources, users can accelerate their learning and mastery of CLI command structures and become proficient in using CLI interfaces for various tasks and operations. In summary, mastering CLI command structures is essential for efficiently navigating and utilizing command-line interfaces to manage and configure systems, applications, and services. By understanding the syntax and structure of CLI commands, mastering command patterns and techniques, familiarizing oneself with available commands and options, and practicing hands-on with CLI environments, users can become proficient in using CLI interfaces effectively and efficiently for various tasks and operations. With continued practice, exploration, and learning, users can further enhance their skills and mastery of CLI command structures, enabling them to leverage the full power and flexibility of command-line interfaces in their daily workflows and operations. Advanced parameter usage and command options play a pivotal role in maximizing the efficiency and effectiveness of command-line interfaces, allowing users to tailor commands to their specific requirements and achieve desired outcomes with precision and flexibility. Command options, also known as flags or switches, modify the behavior of CLI commands by enabling users to specify additional settings, parameters, or actions. Understanding and mastering advanced parameter usage and command options empower users to leverage the full capabilities of CLI tools and utilities, enabling them to perform complex tasks and operations more efficiently and effectively. One of the key aspects of advanced parameter usage is understanding the different types* of command options and their functionalities. CLI commands often support various types of options, including boolean options, which enable or disable certain features or behaviors, and value options, which allow users to specify additional parameters or settings. For example, the command ls -l uses the -l option to enable the long listing format in the ls command, providing detailed information about each file or directory. Additionally, CLI commands may support short and long forms of options, allowing users to specify options using shorthand or more descriptive names. For example, the command ls -a and ls --all both enable the display of hidden files and directories in the ls command, with -a and --all representing short and long forms of the all option, respectively. Moreover, mastering advanced parameter usage involves understanding how to combine multiple options and parameters to create complex command sequences or pipelines that achieve specific objectives. Command pipelines allow users to chain multiple commands together, passing the output of one command as input to the next command in the pipeline, enabling users to perform complex data processing or manipulation tasks efficiently. For example, the command cat file.txt | grep "pattern" reads the contents of a file named "file.txt" and passes it to the grep command, which filters the lines containing the specified pattern. By mastering command pipelines and techniques, users can streamline their workflows and perform complex tasks with ease. Furthermore, advanced parameter usage enables users to customize command behavior and output to suit their preferences and requirements. CLI commands often support options for controlling the format, verbosity, and output of command results, allowing users to tailor the command output to their specific needs. For example, the command git log --oneline --graph --decorate customizes the output of the git log command to display a concise summary of commit history with a graphical representation of branching and tags. Additionally, some CLI commands support interactive modes or prompts that guide users through command execution and parameter selection, facilitating interactive and iterative exploration of command options and functionalities. For example, the git add -i command launches the interactive mode for adding files to the Git staging area, allowing users to select files interactively using a menu-based interface. Moreover, mastering advanced parameter usage involves understanding common command patterns and techniques used to compose and execute complex command sequences or pipelines. Command pipelines allow users to chain multiple commands together, passing the output of one command as input to the next command in the pipeline, enabling users to perform complex data processing or manipulation tasks efficiently. For example, the command cat file.txt | grep "pattern" reads the contents of a file named "file.txt" and passes it to the grep command, which filters the lines containing the specified pattern.

By mastering command pipelines and techniques, users can streamline their workflows and perform complex tasks with ease. Additionally, mastering advanced parameter usage enables users to optimize command performance and resource utilization by fine-tuning command options and parameters to suit specific requirements and constraints. CLI commands often support options for controlling resource allocation, concurrency, and parallelism, allowing users to optimize command execution and resource utilization for improved performance and efficiency. For example, the command npm install --production --no-optional installs Node.js dependencies in production mode without installing optional packages, reducing the installation time and disk space usage. Moreover, mastering advanced parameter usage involves understanding how to troubleshoot common errors or issues that may arise when using command options and parameters. CLI commands may produce error messages or unexpected results if command options are used incorrectly or conflicts arise between different options. By familiarizing themselves with command syntax, conventions, and error handling mechanisms, users can diagnose and resolve issues effectively, ensuring smooth and error-free command execution. In summary, mastering advanced parameter usage and command options is essential for maximizing the efficiency, flexibility, and effectiveness of command-line interfaces. By understanding the different types of options, combining multiple options and parameters, customizing command behavior and output, and troubleshooting common errors, users can leverage the full capabilities of CLI tools and utilities to perform complex tasks and operations with precision and confidence. With continued practice, exploration, and learning, users can further enhance their skills and mastery of advanced parameter usage, enabling them to optimize command performance, streamline workflows, and achieve desired outcomes more efficiently and effectively.

Chapter 2: Automating Networking Tasks with Azure CLI

Scripting automation workflows with Azure CLI is a fundamental aspect of efficiently managing and orchestrating cloud resources and services in Azure environments, enabling users to automate repetitive tasks, streamline workflows, and increase productivity. Azure CLI provides a powerful and flexible command-line interface for managing Azure resources and services, allowing users to interact with Azure programmatically using scripts and automation tools. By mastering scripting techniques and automation workflows with Azure CLI, users can automate a wide range of tasks and operations, such as resource provisioning, configuration management, deployment orchestration, and monitoring automation. One of the key benefits of scripting automation workflows with Azure CLI is the ability to automate repetitive and time-consuming tasks, reducing manual intervention and human errors, and improving operational efficiency and consistency. With Azure CLI, users can create scripts that execute sequences of CLI commands to perform complex tasks and operations automatically, eliminating the need for manual intervention and enabling consistent and repeatable execution of tasks. For example, the command az vm create creates a new virtual machine

(VM) in Azure, specifying parameters such as VM name, resource group, virtual network, and operating system image, allowing users to provision VMs programmatically using scripts. Additionally, users can leverage scripting techniques such as loops, conditionals, and error handling to create robust and resilient automation workflows that adapt to changing conditions and requirements. For example, users can use Bash or PowerShell scripting to iterate over a list of resources and perform actions based on specific conditions, such as resource status or metadata. By incorporating scripting techniques into automation workflows, users can create dynamic and flexible automation solutions that automate complex tasks and adapt to evolving business needs and requirements. Furthermore, scripting automation workflows with Azure CLI enables users to orchestrate deployment and configuration processes for Azure resources and services, facilitating the rapid and consistent provisioning of infrastructure and applications in Azure environments. Users can create deployment scripts that automate the deployment of entire application stacks, including virtual machines, databases, storage accounts, and networking resources, using Azure Resource Manager (ARM) templates or Azure CLI commands. For example, users can use ARM templates to define the infrastructure and configuration of an application stack in a declarative manner, and then use Azure CLI commands to deploy the template and provision the

resources automatically. By automating deployment and configuration processes with Azure CLI, users can accelerate the time-to-market for applications, reduce manual errors, and ensure consistency and compliance with organizational standards and policies. Moreover, scripting automation workflows with Azure CLI enables users to integrate Azure CLI commands into existing automation tools and frameworks, such as CI/CD pipelines, configuration management systems, and DevOps workflows, enabling seamless integration and interoperability with other tools and processes. Users can invoke Azure CLI commands from scripting languages such as Bash, PowerShell, Python, or JavaScript, allowing them to leverage Azure CLI capabilities within their preferred automation environment. For example, users can use Azure CLI commands in Jenkins pipelines to automate the deployment of applications to Azure, or integrate Azure CLI commands with Ansible playbooks to automate configuration management tasks across Azure resources. By integrating Azure CLI commands into existing automation workflows, users can leverage the capabilities of Azure CLI alongside other automation tools and processes, enabling end-to-end automation of complex workflows and operations. Additionally, scripting automation workflows with Azure CLI enables users to implement advanced automation scenarios, such as dynamic scaling, self-healing, and cost optimization, by leveraging Azure CLI commands in combination with

Azure services such as Azure Automation, Azure Functions, and Azure Logic Apps. Users can create automation scripts that monitor resource usage metrics, detect anomalies or thresholds, and trigger automated actions or remediation tasks using Azure CLI commands. For example, users can use Azure CLI commands to scale virtual machine instances based on CPU utilization metrics, or automatically resize storage volumes based on storage usage thresholds. By combining Azure CLI commands with Azure services and automation capabilities, users can implement advanced automation workflows that optimize resource utilization, improve scalability, and reduce operational overhead. In summary, scripting automation workflows with Azure CLI is a powerful and essential skill for efficiently managing and orchestrating cloud resources and services in Azure environments. By mastering scripting techniques and automation workflows with Azure CLI, users can automate repetitive tasks, streamline workflows, and increase productivity, enabling them to achieve greater efficiency, agility, and scalability in their Azure deployments. With the flexibility and extensibility of Azure CLI, users can create robust and resilient automation solutions that adapt to changing conditions and requirements, enabling them to optimize resource utilization, improve operational efficiency, and drive business value in Azure environments.

Building custom CLI scripts for networking operations

is a crucial skill for effectively managing and automating networking tasks and configurations in diverse environments, enabling users to tailor CLI commands to their specific requirements and streamline network management workflows. Custom CLI scripts empower users to automate repetitive networking tasks, such as configuring network interfaces, setting up firewall rules, or troubleshooting connectivity issues, by combining multiple CLI commands into reusable scripts that execute predefined sequences of actions. By mastering the art of building custom CLI scripts, users can leverage the full power and flexibility of CLI tools to automate complex networking operations, increase productivity, and improve operational efficiency. One of the key benefits of building custom CLI scripts for networking operations is the ability to automate repetitive tasks and configurations, reducing manual effort and human errors while ensuring consistency and reliability in network management. With custom CLI scripts, users can automate routine networking tasks such as configuring VLANs, assigning IP addresses, or updating routing tables, by defining the necessary CLI commands in a script file and executing them sequentially. For example, users can create a Bash script that configures network interfaces on multiple servers simultaneously using the ifconfig or ip command, specifying parameters such as interface names, IP addresses, and subnet masks. Additionally, custom CLI scripts enable users to encapsulate complex networking configurations and operations into simple, executable files that can be easily shared, reused, and modified as needed. By organizing CLI commands into logical sequences and encapsulating them within scripts, users can create reusable building blocks for automating common networking tasks and operations, saving time and effort in network management. For example, users can create a PowerShell script that configures firewall rules on Azure virtual machines using the New-AzFirewallRule cmdlet, specifying parameters such as source IP addresses, destination ports, and action types. Moreover, building custom CLI scripts for networking operations allows users to standardize network configurations and enforce best practices across their infrastructure, ensuring consistency, security, and compliance with organizational policies and standards. By defining standard configurations and templates within CLI scripts, users can ensure that networking resources are provisioned and configured according to predefined guidelines and specifications, reducing the risk of misconfigurations and vulnerabilities in the network infrastructure. For example, users can create an Ansible playbook that deploys consistent network configurations across multiple devices using the ansible-playbook command, specifying parameters such as device inventory, configuration templates, and target groups. Additionally, custom CLI scripts enable users to automate complex networking workflows and *operations that involve multiple steps or dependencies, such as deploying network services, implementing security policies, or troubleshooting connectivity issues. By orchestrating CLI commands within scripts, users can automate end-to-end networking processes and workflows, from initial provisioning to ongoing maintenance and monitoring, enabling them to streamline network operations and improve agility and responsiveness. For example, users can create a Python script that automates the deployment of network services in a cloud environment using the boto3 library, interacting with the AWS CLI to provision virtual private clouds (VPCs), subnets, and security groups programmatically. Furthermore, building custom CLI scripts for networking operations enables users to integrate CLI automation into broader DevOps workflows and toolchains, facilitating seamless collaboration and integration between networking and development teams. By incorporating CLI scripts into CI/CD pipelines, configuration management systems, and orchestration frameworks, users can automate the deployment, configuration, and management of networking resources alongside application code and infrastructure, enabling continuous delivery and deployment of network changes and updates. For example, users can use Jenkins pipelines to automate the deployment of network configurations using custom Groovy scripts that execute CLI commands via SSH or REST APIs, integrating networking operations into the software delivery lifecycle. In summary, building custom CLI scripts for networking operations is a valuable skill for effectively managing and automating networking tasks and configurations in diverse environments. By mastering the art of building custom CLI scripts, users can automate repetitive tasks, standardize network configurations, streamline workflows, and integrate networking operations into broader DevOps workflows and toolchains, enabling them to achieve greater efficiency, agility, and scalability in network management. With the flexibility and extensibility of custom CLI scripts, users can unlock new possibilities for automating complex networking operations and achieving operational excellence in their network infrastructure.*

Chapter 3: Leveraging Azure CLI Extensions for Networking

Installing and managing CLI extensions is a crucial aspect of maximizing the functionality and utility of command-line interfaces, enabling users to extend the capabilities of CLI tools with additional commands, modules, and features tailored to their specific needs and requirements. CLI extensions are packages or plugins that enhance the functionality of CLI tools by providing additional commands, functionalities, or integrations with external services or platforms. By installing and managing CLI extensions, users can customize their CLI environment, streamline workflows, and perform advanced tasks and operations more efficiently. One of the key benefits of installing and managing CLI extensions is the ability to extend the core functionality of CLI tools with specialized commands and features that are not available out-of-the-box. Many CLI tools, such as Azure CLI, AWS CLI, and Git CLI, support the installation of extensions to add new commands or functionalities for specific use cases or scenarios. For example, in Azure CLI, users can install extensions such as azure-cli-iot-ext to manage Internet of Things (IoT) devices or azure-cli-aks to interact with Azure Kubernetes Service (AKS) resources, expanding the range of tasks that can be performed from the command line. Additionally, installing and managing CLI extensions enables users to stay up-to-date with the latest features, improvements, and bug fixes released by the CLI tool's developers and community contributors. CLI extensions are regularly updated and maintained by their respective developers to ensure compatibility with the latest versions of the CLI tool and to incorporate new functionalities or enhancements based on user feedback and evolving requirements. By keeping CLI extensions up-to-date, users can take advantage of new features, improvements, and bug fixes without waiting for the next official release of the CLI tool. For example, users can use the npm command to update Node.js packages, including CLI extensions, to the latest versions available in the npm registry, ensuring that they have access to the latest features and improvements. Moreover, installing and managing CLI extensions allows users to customize their CLI environment to suit their preferences and requirements, tailoring the toolset to their specific workflows, tasks, and use cases. CLI extensions often provide commands or functionalities that are optimized for specific tasks or scenarios, enabling users to perform complex operations more efficiently and effectively. For example, in Git CLI, users can install extensions such as git-flow to streamline the process of using the Git

Flow branching model for software development or git-lfs to manage large files and binary assets more effectively. Additionally, installing and managing CLI extensions enables users to leverage community-contributed plugins and integrations to extend the functionality of CLI tools and integrate them with third-party services or platforms. Many CLI tools have vibrant communities of developers and contributors who create and maintain open-source extensions, plugins, and integrations that enhance the capabilities of the tools and enable users to integrate them with other tools and services in their workflows. By installing community-contributed CLI extensions, users can access a wide range of additional commands, functionalities, and integrations that extend the capabilities of the CLI tool beyond its core features. For example, in VS Code, users can install extensions such as eslint for JavaScript linting or prettier for code formatting, enhancing their coding experience and productivity. Furthermore, installing and managing CLI extensions enables users to share their customizations, configurations, and workflows with others, facilitating collaboration and knowledge sharing within teams and communities. CLI extensions often provide mechanisms for exporting and sharing configurations, settings, and workflows, allowing users to package their customizations into reusable templates or scripts that can be shared with colleagues, collaborators, or the broader community. By sharing CLI extensions and configurations, users can contribute to the collective knowledge and expertise of the community, empowering others to benefit from their insights, best practices, and optimizations. For example, users can create and share zsh shell configurations or bash script templates that automate common tasks or workflows, helping others streamline their CLI experience and productivity. In summary, installing and managing CLI extensions is essential for maximizing the functionality and utility of command-line interfaces, enabling users to extend the capabilities of CLI tools with additional commands, functionalities, and integrations tailored to their specific needs and requirements. By installing and managing CLI extensions, users can customize their CLI environment, stay up-to-date with the latest features and improvements, streamline workflows, and collaborate with others to share customizations, configurations, and workflows. With the flexibility and extensibility of CLI extensions, users can unlock new possibilities for automation, productivity, and innovation in their CLI workflows and operations. Extending networking capabilities with CLI extensions is an essential aspect of enhancing the functionality and flexibility of command-line interfaces for managing and configuring network resources and services. CLI extensions offer additional commands, functionalities, and integrations that augment the core networking capabilities of CLI tools, allowing users to perform advanced networking tasks and operations more efficiently and effectively. By leveraging CLI extensions, users can extend the capabilities of CLI tools to interact with a wide range of networking components, protocols, and services, enabling them to build and manage complex network infrastructures with ease. One of the key benefits of extending networking capabilities with CLI extensions is the ability to access specialized commands and functionalities that are tailored to specific networking scenarios or use cases. CLI extensions provide additional commands that are not available in the core set of commands included with the CLI tool, allowing users to perform advanced networking tasks such as configuring virtual private networks (VPNs), setting up load balancers, or managing network security policies. For example, in Azure CLI, users can install extensions such as azure-cli-network to access additional commands for managing Azure networking resources such as virtual networks, subnets, and network security groups, expanding the range of networking tasks that can be performed from the command line. Additionally, extending networking capabilities with CLI extensions enables users to integrate CLI tools with third-party networking platforms, services, and APIs, allowing them to leverage the functionality of external networking solutions within their CLI workflows. CLI extensions often provide integrations with popular networking platforms and services, enabling users to interact with these platforms programmatically from the command line. For example, users can install extensions such as aws-cli to interact with Amazon Web Services (AWS) networking resources, gcloud to interact with Google Cloud networking resources, or kubectl to interact with Kubernetes networking resources, extending the reach of CLI tools beyond their native capabilities. Moreover, extending networking capabilities with CLI extensions allows users to automate networking tasks and operations through scripting and automation workflows, enabling them to streamline network management processes and improve operational efficiency. CLI extensions provide additional commands and functionalities that can be incorporated into scripts and automation workflows to automate repetitive networking tasks such as provisioning virtual networks, configuring network security policies, or monitoring network performance. For example, users can create Bash or PowerShell scripts that leverage CLI extensions to automate the deployment and configuration of networking resources in cloud environments, reducing manual effort and human errors. Furthermore, extending networking capabilities with CLI extensions enables users to customize their CLI environment to suit their preferences and requirements, tailoring the toolset to their specific networking workflows and use cases. CLI extensions often provide options for configuring and customizing the behavior of networking commands and functionalities, allowing users to adapt the toolset to their unique networking requirements. For example, users can customize CLI extensions to support specific networking protocols, standards, or configurations, enabling them to perform tasks such as configuring routing protocols, managing VLANs, or setting up firewall rules according to their organization's networking policies. Additionally, extending networking capabilities with CLI extensions enables users to stay up-to-date with the latest networking features, improvements, and bug fixes released by the developers and community contributors of the CLI tools. CLI extensions are regularly updated and maintained to ensure compatibility with the latest versions of the CLI tools and to incorporate new functionalities or enhancements based on user feedback and evolving networking requirements. By keeping CLI extensions up-to-date, users can take advantage of new features, improvements, and bug fixes without waiting for the next official release of *the CLI tool. In summary, extending networking capabilities with CLI extensions is essential for enhancing the functionality, flexibility, and efficiency of command-line interfaces for managing and configuring network resources and services. By leveraging CLI extensions, users can access specialized commands, integrations, and automation capabilities that enable them to perform advanced networking tasks, integrate with third-party networking platforms, automate networking operations, customize their CLI environment, and stay up-to-date with the latest networking features and improvements. With the flexibility and extensibility of CLI extensions, users can unlock new possibilities for managing and configuring network infrastructures effectively and efficiently from the command line.*

Chapter 4: Advanced Virtual Network Configuration with CLI

Dynamic virtual network scaling techniques are crucial for optimizing network performance, ensuring scalability, and adapting to changing workload demands in cloud environments, allowing users to dynamically adjust the size and capacity of virtual networks to meet evolving requirements and conditions. Dynamic scaling techniques enable users to automatically adjust the number of network resources, such as virtual machines, subnets, and IP addresses, in response to changes in network traffic, workload patterns, or resource utilization, ensuring optimal performance and efficiency while minimizing costs and resource wastage. One of the key techniques for dynamic virtual network scaling is autoscaling, which allows users to automatically adjust the capacity of virtual network resources based on predefined metrics or thresholds, such as CPU utilization, network throughput, or request latency. Autoscaling enables users to scale resources up or down in real-time to handle fluctuations in workload demand, ensuring that network performance remains consistent and responsive under varying conditions. In cloud environments, autoscaling can be implemented using built-in features provided by cloud providers, such as Azure Autoscale in Microsoft Azure, AWS Auto

Scaling in Amazon Web Services, or Google Cloud Autoscaler in Google Cloud Platform. These services allow users to define scaling policies that specify when and how to scale network resources based on metrics collected from monitoring services or telemetry data. For example, users can use the az monitor autoscale command in Azure CLI to create autoscaling rules that scale virtual machine instances based on CPU utilization metrics, specifying parameters such as scaling thresholds, cooldown periods, and minimum and maximum instance counts. Additionally, dynamic virtual network scaling techniques can leverage predictive scaling algorithms that use historical data and machine learning models to forecast future workload patterns and anticipate resource requirements, enabling proactive scaling actions to be taken in advance of anticipated demand spikes or capacity constraints. Predictive scaling techniques analyze historical workload data, such as traffic patterns, request rates, or resource utilization trends, to identify recurring patterns and trends that can be used to predict future workload patterns and adjust network resources accordingly. For example, users can use the az monitor metrics list command in Azure CLI to retrieve historical performance data for virtual network resources, such as network bandwidth, packet loss, or latency, and use machine learning algorithms to predict future traffic patterns and adjust resource allocations accordingly. Moreover, dynamic virtual network scaling techniques can incorporate cost optimization strategies to ensure that scaling actions are cost-effective and aligned with budgetary constraints, enabling users to optimize resource utilization while minimizing costs and expenses. Cost optimization techniques focus on maximizing the value of resources by ensuring that scaling actions are triggered only when necessary and that resources are scaled to meet performance requirements at the lowest possible cost. For example, users can use the az consumption command in Azure CLI to monitor resource usage and costs, and use budget alerts or cost management policies to enforce spending limits and optimize resource utilization. Additionally, dynamic virtual network scaling techniques can leverage hybrid cloud architectures and multi-cloud deployments to extend scalability across diverse environments and leverage resources from multiple cloud providers or on-premises data centers. Hybrid cloud and multi-cloud architectures enable users to seamlessly scale network resources across heterogeneous environments, allowing them to leverage the scalability and flexibility of cloud resources while maintaining control and flexibility over their infrastructure and data. For example, users can use Azure Virtual WAN to extend virtual network resources across multiple Azure regions or connect on-premises data centers to Azure using VPN or ExpressRoute connections, enabling seamless scaling and resource allocation across hybrid cloud environments. Furthermore, dynamic virtual network scaling techniques can incorporate automation and orchestration workflows to streamline the process of scaling network resources and automate repetitive tasks, enabling users to deploy, configure, and manage virtual network resources more efficiently and effectively. Automation and orchestration workflows leverage scripting languages, configuration management tools, or orchestration frameworks to automate scaling actions, monitor network performance, and enforce policies and configurations, enabling users to achieve consistent and repeatable results while reducing manual effort and human errors. For example, users can use Azure Automation to create runbooks that automate the process of scaling virtual network resources based on predefined conditions or triggers, such as CPU utilization thresholds or network traffic patterns, enabling proactive scaling actions to be taken automatically without human intervention. In summary, dynamic virtual network scaling techniques are essential for optimizing network performance, ensuring scalability, and adapting to changing workload demands in cloud environments. By leveraging autoscaling, predictive scaling, cost optimization strategies, hybrid cloud architectures, multi-cloud deployments, automation, and orchestration workflows, users can dynamically adjust the size and capacity of virtual networks to meet evolving requirements and conditions while maximizing resource utilization, minimizing costs, and improving operational efficiency and agility. With the flexibility and extensibility of dynamic virtual network scaling techniques, users can achieve optimal performance, scalability, and cost-effectiveness in their network infrastructure, enabling them to meet the demands of modern cloud-native applications and workloads effectively.

Advanced subnet and IP address management is essential for optimizing network resources, ensuring efficient address allocation, and maintaining network security in complex and dynamic environments, enabling users to effectively organize and manage IP address spaces, subnets, and network configurations to meet their specific requirements and objectives. Advanced subnet and IP address management techniques encompass a range of strategies and practices aimed at optimizing the allocation, utilization, and administration of IP addresses and subnets, including subnetting, supernetting, IP address planning, hierarchical addressing schemes, and automation. By applying advanced subnet and IP address management techniques, users can streamline network operations, improve scalability, enhance security, and reduce administrative overhead, allowing them to build and manage robust and resilient network infrastructures. One of the key techniques in advanced subnet and IP address management is subnetting, which involves dividing a larger IP address space into smaller, more manageable subnets to optimize address allocation and network performance. Subnetting enables users to partition a single IP network into multiple smaller subnetworks, each with its own unique subnet address range, subnet mask, and broadcast domain, allowing for more efficient use of IP addresses and improved network segmentation and isolation. For example, users can use the ipcalc command in Linux to calculate subnet masks, network addresses, and broadcast addresses for different subnet configurations based on their requirements, such as the number of hosts per subnet or the desired level of network segmentation. Additionally, advanced subnet and IP address management techniques can incorporate supernetting, which involves aggregating multiple smaller IP address ranges into larger supernets to simplify routing and reduce the size of routing tables, enabling more efficient routing and address summarization. Supernetting allows users to combine multiple contiguous IP address ranges into a single larger address range, reducing the number of routing entries required to represent the address space and improving routing efficiency and scalability. For example, users can use the route command in Linux to add supernet routes to routing tables, specifying the network address and subnet mask of the supernet along with the next-hop router or gateway address. Moreover, advanced subnet and IP address management techniques can include IP address planning, which involves carefully designing and organizing IP address spaces to optimize address allocation, minimize conflicts, and facilitate efficient IP address management and administration. IP address planning encompasses practices such as address space allocation, address assignment policies, IP address assignment methods, and IP address management tools and systems, enabling users to systematically plan, deploy, and manage IP address resources across their network infrastructure. For example, users can use spreadsheet tools or IP address management (IPAM) software solutions to document and manage IP address assignments, allocations, and utilization across different subnets and network segments, ensuring consistency and accuracy in IP address management. Additionally, advanced subnet and IP address management techniques can incorporate hierarchical addressing schemes, which involve organizing IP address spaces in a hierarchical manner to facilitate efficient routing, address summarization, and network management. Hierarchical addressing schemes divide IP address spaces into hierarchical levels, such as regions, sites, subnets, and hosts, allowing for hierarchical aggregation of routing information and more efficient routing and address allocation. For example, users can use hierarchical addressing schemes such as Classless Inter-Domain Routing (CIDR) or Variable Length Subnet Masking (VLSM) to design and manage IP address spaces in a hierarchical manner, enabling more efficient address allocation and routing in large-scale networks. Furthermore, advanced subnet and IP address management techniques can leverage *automation to streamline the process of subnet and IP address provisioning, configuration, and management, enabling users to automate repetitive tasks, enforce consistent policies, and improve operational efficiency and agility. Automation solutions such as scripting, configuration management tools, or IP address management (IPAM) software platforms allow users to automate the deployment, configuration, and management of IP address resources across their network infrastructure, reducing manual effort and human errors. For example, users can use scripting languages such as Python or PowerShell to automate IP address provisioning and configuration tasks, such as subnet creation, IP address assignment, and DNS configuration, using APIs or CLI commands to interact with network devices and systems programmatically. In summary, advanced subnet and IP address management techniques are essential for optimizing network resources, ensuring efficient address allocation, and maintaining network security in complex and dynamic environments. By applying techniques such as subnetting, supernetting, IP address planning, hierarchical addressing schemes, and automation, users can streamline network operations, improve scalability, enhance security, and reduce administrative overhead, enabling them to build and manage robust and resilient network infrastructures effectively. With the right combination of advanced subnet and IP address management techniques, users can achieve optimal performance, efficiency, and reliability in their network environments, ensuring that their IP address resources are utilized effectively and efficiently to meet their business requirements and objectives.*

Chapter 5: Network Security Policies and Advanced Security Configurations

Implementing granular network security policies is crucial for safeguarding network resources, protecting against cyber threats, and ensuring compliance with regulatory requirements in modern IT environments, allowing users to define fine-grained rules and controls to regulate network traffic and access based on specific criteria and conditions. Granular network security policies enable organizations to enforce detailed controls and restrictions at the network level, governing the flow of traffic, defining access privileges, and mitigating risks associated with unauthorized access, data breaches, and malicious activities. By implementing granular network security policies, users can enhance the overall security posture of their network infrastructure, minimize attack surfaces, and mitigate the impact of security incidents and breaches. One of the key techniques in implementing granular network security policies is the use of access control lists (ACLs), which enable users to define rules and filters to permit or deny traffic based on various criteria, such as source and destination IP addresses, ports, protocols, and application types. ACLs allow users to specify fine-

grained controls to restrict access to network resources, block malicious traffic, and enforce security policies at the network perimeter, enabling organizations to control and monitor traffic flow effectively. For example, users can use the iptables command in Linux to configure firewall rules and filter traffic based on source and destination IP addresses, port numbers, and protocol types, allowing only authorized traffic to pass through the firewall while blocking or dropping unauthorized traffic. Additionally, implementing granular network security policies involves the use of network segmentation techniques to divide the network into isolated segments or zones based on trust levels, user roles, or sensitivity of data, enabling organizations to enforce security controls and restrictions at a more granular level. Network segmentation helps contain the spread of threats, limit lateral movement within the network, and minimize the impact of security breaches by isolating critical assets and sensitive data from potential attackers. For example, users can use VLANs (Virtual Local Area Networks) to segment the network into separate broadcast domains based on departmental boundaries or security requirements, ensuring that traffic between different segments is restricted and monitored according to organizational policies. Moreover, implementing granular network security policies involves the use of encryption and tunneling technologies to secure data in transit and protect sensitive information from unauthorized access or interception. Encryption techniques such as IPsec (Internet Protocol Security) and SSL/TLS (Secure Sockets Layer/Transport Layer Security) enable users to establish secure communication channels over untrusted networks, encrypting data packets to prevent eavesdropping and tampering by malicious actors. Tunneling protocols such as VPN (Virtual Private Network) and GRE (Generic Routing Encapsulation) allow users to create secure, private communication channels between remote locations or endpoints, ensuring confidentiality and integrity of data transmitted over public networks. For example, users can use the ipsec command in Linux to configure IPsec VPN tunnels between network devices, encrypting and authenticating traffic between endpoints to establish secure communication channels over the internet or other untrusted networks. Furthermore, implementing granular network security policies involves the use of intrusion detection and prevention systems (IDPS) to detect and mitigate network-based attacks, anomalies, and security breaches in real-time, enabling organizations to identify and respond to security threats proactively. IDPS solutions monitor network traffic for signs of malicious activity, such as suspicious patterns, known attack signatures, or *abnormal behavior, and take immediate action to block or mitigate threats before they can cause harm to the network infrastructure or compromise sensitive data. For example, users can use the snort command in Linux to deploy a network-based intrusion detection system (NIDS) that monitors network traffic for signs of known attack patterns or suspicious activities, generating alerts and taking action to block or quarantine malicious traffic in real-time. Additionally, implementing granular network security policies involves the use of identity and access management (IAM) solutions to authenticate and authorize users, devices, and applications accessing network resources, ensuring that only authorized entities are granted access to sensitive data and critical systems. IAM solutions enable organizations to enforce policies and controls based on user identities, roles, and permissions, and to track and audit access to network resources to detect and prevent unauthorized activities. For example, users can use the Active Directory command in Windows Server to configure user accounts, groups, and permissions, and to enforce access controls and restrictions based on user roles and organizational policies. In summary, implementing granular network security policies is essential for protecting network resources, mitigating cyber threats, and ensuring compliance with regulatory requirements in modern IT environments. By leveraging techniques such as access control lists (ACLs), network segmentation, encryption, tunneling, intrusion detection and prevention systems (IDPS), and identity and access management (IAM) solutions, organizations can enforce fine-grained controls and restrictions to regulate network traffic, secure data in transit, detect and mitigate security threats, and authenticate and authorize users accessing network resources effectively. With the right combination of granular network security policies and technologies, organizations can strengthen their overall security posture, minimize risks, and safeguard their network infrastructure against evolving cyber threats and attacks.*

Advanced Threat Protection Strategies with CLI are indispensable for fortifying cybersecurity postures, thwarting sophisticated cyber threats, and safeguarding sensitive data in today's digital landscape, empowering users to deploy proactive measures and countermeasures to detect, mitigate, and respond to advanced threats and attacks effectively. Advanced Threat Protection (ATP) strategies encompass a diverse array of techniques and methodologies aimed at identifying, analyzing, and mitigating advanced cyber threats, including malware, ransomware, phishing, zero-day exploits, and insider threats, leveraging CLI commands to orchestrate security defenses, analyze security events, and enforce security policies across diverse IT environments. By adopting advanced threat protection strategies with CLI, organizations can bolster their resilience against evolving cyber threats, enhance incident response capabilities, and minimize the impact of security breaches and data breaches on their operations and reputation. One of the key techniques in advanced threat protection strategies with CLI is leveraging threat intelligence feeds and threat detection tools to gather actionable intelligence about emerging cyber threats, adversary tactics, and attack trends, enabling organizations to stay ahead of adversaries and proactively defend against potential threats. Threat intelligence feeds provide valuable insights into known indicators of compromise (IOCs), suspicious activities, and malicious domains or IP addresses, allowing security teams to enrich security logs, correlate security events, and identify potential security incidents more effectively. For example, users can use the az security command in Azure CLI to integrate threat intelligence feeds from sources such as Microsoft Threat Intelligence Center (MSTIC) or third-party threat intelligence providers, enabling organizations to enrich security alerts and enhance threat detection capabilities based on real-time intelligence about emerging threats and vulnerabilities. Additionally, advanced threat protection strategies with CLI involve implementing endpoint detection and response (EDR) solutions to monitor and analyze endpoint activities, detect anomalous behavior, and respond to security incidents in real-time, enabling organizations to identify and mitigate threats targeting endpoints, such as desktops, laptops, servers, and mobile devices. EDR solutions provide visibility into endpoint activities, collect telemetry data, and apply machine learning algorithms and behavioral analytics to detect suspicious behavior indicative of compromise or malicious activity, allowing security teams to respond promptly and effectively to security incidents. For example, users can use the az monitor command in Azure CLI to deploy Azure Security Center (ASC) agents on endpoints and servers, enabling organizations to monitor and analyze endpoint activities, detect potential security threats, and respond to incidents using built-in EDR capabilities and threat intelligence integration. Moreover, advanced threat protection strategies with CLI encompass implementing network traffic analysis (NTA) solutions to monitor and analyze network traffic patterns, detect suspicious activities, and identify potential security threats in real-time, enabling organizations to detect and mitigate network-based attacks, such as intrusions, data exfiltration, and command and control communications. NTA solutions leverage packet capture and analysis techniques, deep packet inspection, and machine learning algorithms to monitor network traffic, identify anomalous behavior, and correlate security events to detect and respond to security incidents effectively. For example, users can use the az network command in Azure CLI to deploy Azure Network Watcher to monitor network traffic, analyze network flows, and detect potential security threats based on predefined security rules and anomaly detection algorithms. Furthermore, advanced threat protection strategies with CLI involve implementing security information and event management (SIEM) solutions to aggregate, correlate, and analyze security logs and events from across the IT environment, enabling organizations to gain visibility into security incidents, streamline incident response workflows, and facilitate compliance with regulatory requirements. SIEM solutions collect log data from various sources, such as endpoints, servers, network devices, and security appliances, and apply correlation rules, threat intelligence feeds, and behavioral analytics to identify and prioritize security incidents based on severity and impact. For example, users can use the az monitor log-analytics command in Azure CLI to deploy Azure Sentinel, a cloud-native SIEM solution, to collect and analyze security logs and events from Azure resources and on-premises environments, enabling organizations to detect and respond to security *threats effectively using advanced analytics and automation capabilities. In summary, advanced threat protection strategies with CLI are essential for enhancing cybersecurity defenses, mitigating advanced cyber threats, and safeguarding organizations against evolving security risks and challenges. By leveraging threat intelligence feeds, endpoint detection and response (EDR) solutions, network traffic analysis (NTA) tools, and security information and event management (SIEM) platforms with CLI, organizations can detect, analyze, and respond to security incidents more effectively, minimizing the impact of cyber threats on their operations and reputation. With the right combination of advanced threat protection strategies and CLI tools, organizations can strengthen their security posture, improve incident response capabilities, and mitigate the risk of data breaches and security breaches effectively.*

Chapter 6: Scaling and Load Balancing Solutions with CLI

Implementing scalable load balancers with CLI commands is crucial for distributing incoming network traffic across multiple servers or resources, ensuring high availability, fault tolerance, and optimal performance for web applications, APIs, and microservices deployed in cloud environments, enabling users to deploy and manage load balancers programmatically using command-line interfaces to automate the configuration and scaling of load balancers based on fluctuating demand and traffic patterns. Load balancers play a critical role in modern IT architectures by evenly distributing incoming requests across multiple backend servers or instances, allowing organizations to scale their applications horizontally, handle increased traffic loads, and improve application responsiveness and reliability. By implementing scalable load balancers with CLI commands, organizations can achieve greater flexibility, scalability, and cost efficiency in managing their application workloads and delivering seamless user experiences to their customers and end-users. One of the key techniques in implementing scalable load balancers with CLI commands is deploying load balancers using infrastructure-as-code (IaC) principles and configuration management tools to define and provision load balancer resources as code, enabling users to automate the deployment and configuration of load balancers alongside other infrastructure components using declarative templates or scripts. IaC tools such as Terraform, Ansible, or Azure Resource Manager (ARM) templates allow users to describe load balancer configurations, backend pools, health probes, and routing rules in a human-readable format, and deploy them consistently across different environments, ensuring consistency and reproducibility in load balancer deployments. For example, users can use the az network lb command in Azure CLI to deploy Azure Load Balancer resources, specifying parameters such as backend pool configurations, load balancing rules, health probe settings, and frontend IP configurations to define the behavior and routing logic of the load balancer. Additionally, implementing scalable load balancers with CLI commands involves configuring auto-scaling policies and dynamic scaling mechanisms to automatically adjust the capacity of load balancers based on changes in demand, traffic patterns, or resource utilization metrics, enabling organizations to scale their load balancer resources up or down in real-time to accommodate fluctuations in workload and traffic volume. Auto-scaling policies allow users to define thresholds or conditions for scaling actions, such as increasing or decreasing the number of backend servers or adjusting the capacity of load balancer instances, based on metrics such as CPU utilization, network throughput, or request latency. For example, users can use the az monitor autoscale command in Azure CLI to configure auto-scaling rules for Azure Load Balancer resources, specifying conditions such as CPU utilization thresholds or request count thresholds, and defining scaling actions such as adding or removing backend servers from the load balancer pool dynamically based on workload metrics. Moreover, implementing scalable load balancers with CLI commands involves integrating load balancers with container orchestration platforms such as Kubernetes or Docker Swarm to manage and scale containerized workloads more efficiently, enabling organizations to leverage container-based architectures and microservices deployments while ensuring high availability and fault tolerance for their applications. Container orchestration platforms provide built-in support for load balancing and service discovery, allowing users to deploy and manage load balancers alongside containerized services using declarative YAML manifests or CLI commands, and automate the scaling and load distribution of containerized workloads based on resource utilization or custom metrics. For example, users can use the kubectl command in Kubernetes to create and manage Kubernetes Services of type LoadBalancer, specifying parameters such as service ports, backend pod selectors, and load balancing algorithms to define the behavior and routing logic of the Kubernetes load balancer, and automatically expose containerized services to external clients or applications. Furthermore, implementing scalable load balancers with CLI commands involves configuring health checks and monitoring solutions to monitor the health and availability of backend servers or resources, enabling organizations to detect and remediate issues proactively, and ensure continuous availability and reliability of their applications and services. Health checks allow load balancers to periodically probe backend servers or endpoints to verify their health status and responsiveness, and automatically remove or replace unhealthy servers from the load balancer pool to prevent them from receiving incoming traffic or causing service disruptions. For example, users can use the az network lb probe command in Azure CLI to configure health probes for Azure Load Balancer resources, specifying parameters such as probe protocols, intervals, timeouts, and thresholds to define the criteria for determining the health status of backend servers, and automatically failover or scale out load balancer resources based on health probe results. In summary, implementing scalable load balancers with CLI commands is essential for distributing incoming network traffic across multiple servers or resources, ensuring high availability, fault tolerance, and optimal performance for web applications, APIs, and microservices deployed in cloud environments. By leveraging infrastructure-as-code (IaC) principles, auto-scaling policies, container orchestration platforms, and health checks, organizations can deploy and manage load balancers programmatically, automate the scaling and load distribution of their application workloads, and ensure continuous availability and reliability of their services, enabling them to deliver seamless user experiences and meet the demands of their customers and end-users effectively.

Advanced traffic management and routing techniques are indispensable for optimizing network performance, ensuring high availability, and enhancing the reliability of applications and services deployed in cloud environments, enabling users to leverage advanced routing protocols, traffic shaping mechanisms, and traffic management policies to intelligently route and prioritize network traffic based on specific criteria and conditions, facilitating efficient resource utilization, load balancing, and fault tolerance across distributed IT infrastructures. Advanced traffic management and routing techniques encompass a diverse range of strategies and methodologies aimed at optimizing the flow of network traffic, improving application responsiveness, and minimizing latency and packet loss, leveraging CLI commands to configure and manage routing tables, traffic policies, and Quality of Service (QoS) parameters programmatically to achieve desired performance objectives and service levels. By implementing advanced traffic management and routing techniques with CLI commands, organizations can achieve greater flexibility, scalability, and control over their network infrastructure, enabling them to adapt to changing traffic patterns, mitigate congestion, and deliver superior user experiences to their customers and end-users. One of the key techniques in advanced traffic management and routing is leveraging dynamic routing protocols such as BGP (Border Gateway Protocol) or OSPF (Open Shortest Path First) to dynamically exchange routing information and calculate optimal paths for network traffic based on factors such as network topology, link bandwidth, and path cost. Dynamic routing protocols enable routers and switches to automatically discover and adapt to changes in network topology or link conditions, allowing organizations to achieve efficient and reliable communication between network segments, data centers, or cloud regions. For example, users can use the bgp command in Cisco IOS to configure BGP peering sessions, advertise network prefixes, and apply route policies to influence the selection of best paths for outgoing traffic, ensuring optimal routing and load balancing across multiple network paths. Additionally, implementing advanced traffic management and routing involves deploying traffic shaping and traffic engineering techniques to control the flow of network traffic, prioritize critical applications, and allocate bandwidth resources effectively, enabling organizations to enforce traffic policies, QoS parameters, and service-level agreements (SLAs) to meet performance objectives and user expectations. Traffic shaping mechanisms such as rate limiting, traffic prioritization, and congestion management allow organizations to regulate the transmission of network packets, prevent network congestion, and ensure fair distribution of bandwidth resources among competing applications and users. For example, users can use the tc command in Linux to configure traffic control policies, classify traffic flows using packet filters or classifiers, and apply queuing disciplines such as Hierarchical Token Bucket (HTB) or Stochastic Fairness Queueing (SFQ) to shape and prioritize network traffic based on predefined rules and criteria, ensuring optimal performance and resource utilization. Moreover, implementing advanced traffic management and routing involves deploying intelligent load balancing solutions to distribute incoming network traffic across multiple servers, instances, or endpoints based on factors such as server capacity, workload, and geographic proximity, enabling organizations to achieve high availability, fault tolerance, and scalability for their applications and services. Load balancing algorithms such as Round Robin, Least Connections, or Weighted Round Robin allow organizations to evenly distribute incoming requests among backend servers or instances, optimize resource utilization, and ensure that no single server or resource is overwhelmed by excessive traffic. For example, users can use the ipvsadm command in Linux to configure IPVS (IP Virtual Server) load balancer rules, define backend server pools, and specify load balancing algorithms and scheduling policies to distribute incoming traffic across multiple backend servers or instances based on predefined criteria and conditions, ensuring optimal performance and availability for web applications, APIs, or microservices. Furthermore, implementing advanced traffic management and routing involves deploying traffic monitoring and analytics solutions to collect, analyze, and visualize network traffic data in real-time, enabling organizations to gain insights into traffic patterns, identify performance bottlenecks, and troubleshoot network issues proactively. Traffic monitoring tools such as Wireshark, tcpdump, or Prometheus allow organizations to capture and analyze network packets, monitor network utilization, and detect anomalies or irregularities in traffic behavior, facilitating timely decision-making and remediation actions to optimize network performance and reliability. For example, users can use the wireshark command in Linux to capture and analyze network packets, filter traffic based on specific criteria or protocols, and identify potential performance issues or security threats affecting network communication, enabling organizations to diagnose and resolve network problems effectively. In summary, implementing advanced traffic management and routing techniques with CLI commands is essential for optimizing network performance, ensuring high availability, and enhancing the reliability of applications and services deployed in cloud environments. By leveraging dynamic routing protocols, traffic shaping mechanisms, intelligent load balancing solutions, and traffic monitoring tools, organizations can achieve greater control and visibility over their network infrastructure, adapt to changing traffic patterns, and deliver superior user experiences to their customers and end-users, enabling them to meet their performance objectives and business goals effectively.

Chapter 7: Advanced Network Monitoring and Logging Techniques

Customizing network monitoring dashboards is essential for organizations to gain comprehensive insights into the performance, health, and security of their network infrastructure, enabling users to tailor monitoring dashboards to their specific requirements, visualize key performance indicators (KPIs), and identify trends or anomalies in network traffic and behavior effectively. Network monitoring dashboards serve as centralized platforms for monitoring and analyzing network-related metrics, events, and alerts, allowing organizations to track the availability, utilization, and reliability of network devices, services, and connections in real-time, facilitating proactive troubleshooting, capacity planning, and optimization of network resources. By customizing network monitoring dashboards, organizations can configure personalized views, charts, and reports to monitor critical network parameters, visualize data trends, and streamline decision-making processes, enabling them to monitor and manage their network infrastructure more effectively and efficiently. One of the key techniques in customizing network monitoring dashboards is leveraging monitoring and visualization tools such as Grafana, Kibana, or Microsoft Azure Monitor to design and deploy custom dashboards that meet specific monitoring requirements and objectives. These tools provide intuitive interfaces, drag-and-drop editors, and pre-built visualization components that allow users to create, modify, and customize dashboards easily, without the need for extensive coding or programming skills. For example, users can use the grafana-cli command to install Grafana on a Linux server, configure data sources such as Prometheus or InfluxDB to collect network metrics, and create custom dashboards using Grafana's web-based interface, allowing them to visualize network performance metrics such as bandwidth utilization, packet loss, and latency in real-time. Additionally, customizing network monitoring dashboards involves selecting and configuring relevant data sources, metrics, and visualization widgets to display key network performance indicators and status information effectively. Users can leverage built-in data sources such as SNMP (Simple Network Management Protocol), NetFlow, or Syslog to collect network metrics and events from routers, switches, firewalls, and other network devices, and configure dashboard panels such as line charts, bar graphs, or heatmaps to visualize network performance metrics such as throughput, error rates, and interface utilization over time. For example, users can use the snmp-exporter command to deploy an SNMP exporter on a Linux server, configure SNMP polling for network devices such as routers or switches, and scrape SNMP metrics using Prometheus, enabling them to visualize network performance metrics on custom dashboards using Grafana's Prometheus data source integration. Moreover, customizing network monitoring dashboards involves designing and organizing dashboard layouts and widgets to provide meaningful insights and actionable information to users, enabling them to monitor and troubleshoot network issues effectively. Users can arrange dashboard panels into logical groups, organize them hierarchically, and add annotations, thresholds, or alerts to highlight important events or anomalies in network traffic or performance. For example, users can use the grafana-cli command to create a new dashboard in Grafana, add panels such as line charts or gauges to visualize network metrics, and configure alert rules to notify administrators via email or Slack when network performance exceeds predefined thresholds or criteria, enabling them to respond to network issues promptly and minimize downtime or service disruptions. Furthermore, customizing network monitoring dashboards involves integrating third-party data sources and external systems to enrich dashboard content and context, enabling users to correlate network performance metrics with application performance, infrastructure changes, or business metrics to gain holistic insights into overall system health and performance. Users can leverage APIs, webhooks, or data ingestion mechanisms to ingest data from external sources such as application performance monitoring (APM) tools, cloud platforms, or ticketing systems, and integrate them into custom dashboards to provide end-to-end visibility and context-aware monitoring capabilities. For example, users can use the curl command to fetch data from external APIs such as the Azure Monitor REST API, parse JSON responses using tools like jq, and ingest the data into Grafana using the SimpleJson data source plugin, allowing them to create unified dashboards that display network metrics alongside application performance data or service health status, enabling them to correlate and analyze data more effectively. In summary, customizing network monitoring dashboards is essential for organizations to gain comprehensive insights into the performance, health, and security of their network infrastructure, enabling them to monitor and manage their network resources more effectively and efficiently. By leveraging monitoring and visualization tools, configuring relevant data sources and metrics, designing intuitive layouts and widgets, and integrating third-party data sources, organizations can create personalized dashboards that provide actionable insights and enable proactive monitoring, troubleshooting, and optimization of their network infrastructure, empowering them to deliver superior network performance and reliability to their users and customers.

Analyzing network logs for performance optimization is a critical aspect of maintaining a healthy and efficient network infrastructure, enabling organizations to identify and address bottlenecks, anomalies, and inefficiencies that may impact network performance and user experience negatively. Network logs contain valuable information about network traffic, communication patterns, errors, and anomalies, allowing administrators to gain insights into the behavior and health of their network environment, facilitating proactive troubleshooting, capacity planning, and optimization efforts. By leveraging log analysis tools and techniques, organizations can parse, visualize, and interpret network logs effectively, enabling them to identify performance issues, diagnose root causes, and implement targeted optimizations to improve network performance and reliability. One of the key techniques in analyzing network logs for performance optimization is using log aggregation and analysis platforms such as Elasticsearch, Logstash, and Kibana (ELK stack) to collect, centralize, and analyze log data from multiple sources, including routers, switches, firewalls, servers, and applications, allowing administrators to correlate events, detect patterns, and gain actionable insights into network performance and behavior. These platforms provide powerful querying capabilities, visualization tools, and alerting mechanisms that enable administrators to search, filter, and analyze log data in real-time, facilitating rapid identification and resolution of network issues. For example, users can use the docker-compose command to deploy an ELK stack containerized environment on a Docker host, configure Logstash to ingest network logs from syslog or other log sources, and create custom dashboards in Kibana to visualize network performance metrics such as bandwidth utilization, packet loss, and latency, enabling them to monitor and optimize network performance effectively. Additionally, analyzing network logs for performance optimization involves defining and monitoring key performance indicators (KPIs) and metrics that are relevant to network performance and user experience, enabling administrators to track and measure the performance of their network infrastructure against predefined objectives and thresholds. Common network performance metrics include latency, throughput, packet loss, error rates, and network utilization, which can be monitored and analyzed using log analysis tools to identify deviations from normal behavior and performance benchmarks. For example, administrators can use the tcpdump command to capture network traffic on specific interfaces or ports, filter traffic based on protocol or source/destination IP addresses, and analyze packet headers to measure round-trip times (RTT), detect retransmissions, or identify network congestion points, enabling them to diagnose and troubleshoot performance issues effectively. Moreover, analyzing network logs for performance optimization involves using machine learning and anomaly detection techniques to identify abnormal patterns or behaviors in network traffic, enabling administrators to detect security threats, performance anomalies, and configuration errors that may impact network performance and reliability. Machine learning algorithms such as clustering, classification, and anomaly detection can be trained on historical network log data to identify patterns and trends, and predict future network behavior, enabling administrators to proactively identify and address performance issues before they impact users or applications. For example, administrators can use the scikit-learn library in Python to train a machine learning model on historical network log data, extract features such as traffic volume, protocol distribution, and communication patterns, and use anomaly detection algorithms such as isolation forests or k-means clustering to identify unusual network behavior or outliers, enabling them to prioritize and remediate performance issues effectively. Furthermore, analyzing network logs for performance optimization involves integrating log analysis with other monitoring and management tools such as network performance monitoring (NPM) systems, application performance monitoring (APM) solutions, and configuration management databases (CMDBs) to provide end-to-end visibility and context-aware insights into network performance and behavior. By integrating log analysis with other monitoring tools and data sources, administrators can correlate network events with application performance metrics, infrastructure changes, and business operations, enabling them to gain holistic insights into overall system health and performance, and make data-driven decisions to optimize network performance and reliability. For example, administrators can use the curl command to fetch performance data from an APM tool's API, parse JSON responses using tools like jq, and ingest the data into Elasticsearch using Logstash, enabling them to correlate application performance metrics such as response times, error rates, and transaction volumes with network log data to identify performance bottlenecks and optimize network infrastructure accordingly. In summary, analyzing network logs for performance optimization is a crucial aspect of maintaining a *healthy and efficient network infrastructure, enabling organizations to identify and address performance issues, diagnose root causes, and implement targeted optimizations to improve network performance and reliability. By leveraging log analysis tools and techniques, defining and monitoring key performance indicators, using machine learning and anomaly detection, and integrating log analysis with other monitoring tools and data sources, administrators can gain comprehensive insights into network performance and behavior, and optimize network infrastructure to meet the demands of users and applications effectively.*

Chapter 8: Implementing High Availability Architectures

Designing redundant networking architectures with CLI commands is essential for ensuring high availability, fault tolerance, and resilience in modern IT infrastructures, allowing organizations to minimize the risk of network downtime and service disruptions by implementing redundant components, paths, and failover mechanisms. Redundant networking architectures are designed to eliminate single points of failure and mitigate the impact of hardware failures, software bugs, or human errors that may occur in network infrastructure, enabling organizations to maintain uninterrupted access to critical resources and services even in the event of failures or disruptions. By leveraging CLI commands to configure redundant networking architectures, organizations can implement redundancy at various layers of the network stack, including physical connectivity, network protocols, and application services, to enhance reliability and performance and meet stringent service level agreements (SLAs) and business continuity requirements effectively. One of the key techniques in designing redundant networking architectures with CLI commands is implementing redundant physical connectivity using technologies such as link aggregation (LACP) or redundant trunking

(802.3ad), which allow organizations to combine multiple physical links into a single logical link to increase bandwidth and provide failover capabilities. By configuring link aggregation groups (LAGs) or EtherChannels using CLI commands, administrators can bond together multiple network interfaces on switches, routers, or servers, enabling them to create redundant paths between network devices and distribute traffic evenly across available links, ensuring that network connectivity remains resilient and highly available even if individual links or devices fail. For example, administrators can use the interface port-channel command on Cisco switches to create a port-channel interface, add member interfaces to the port-channel group using the channel-group command, and configure LACP parameters such as mode and timers to negotiate link aggregation with connected devices, enabling them to establish redundant links and load balance traffic effectively. Additionally, designing redundant networking architectures with CLI commands involves implementing redundant routing protocols such as HSRP (Hot Standby Router Protocol), VRRP (Virtual Router Redundancy Protocol), or OSPF (Open Shortest Path First), which enable organizations to maintain continuous network connectivity and routing functionality by electing backup routers or gateways to take over traffic forwarding in the event of primary router failure. By configuring redundant routing protocols using CLI commands, administrators can ensure seamless

failover and failback operations, monitor the health and status of router redundancy groups, and optimize routing paths dynamically to improve network performance and resilience. For example, administrators can use the router ospf command on Cisco routers to enable OSPF routing, configure redundant OSPF adjacency with backup routers using the backup interface command, and adjust OSPF cost metrics or priority values to influence route selection and failover behavior, enabling them to design redundant routing architectures that maximize network availability and resilience. Moreover, designing redundant networking architectures with CLI commands involves implementing redundant network services and applications using technologies such as load balancing, clustering, or virtualization, which enable organizations to distribute workloads across multiple servers or instances and provide failover capabilities for critical services and applications. By configuring redundant network services using CLI commands, administrators can deploy redundant instances of application servers, databases, or virtual machines, configure load balancers or clustering software to distribute incoming traffic and workload evenly, and monitor service health and availability to ensure continuous operation and high availability. For example, administrators can use the ipvsadm command on Linux servers to configure IPVS (IP Virtual Server) load balancer rules, define backend server pools, and specify load balancing algorithms such as Round Robin or Least Connections to distribute incoming traffic across multiple backend servers, enabling them to design redundant network architectures for web applications, APIs, or microservices that provide seamless failover and scalability. In summary, designing redundant networking architectures with CLI commands is essential for ensuring high availability, fault tolerance, and resilience in modern IT infrastructures, enabling organizations to minimize the risk of network downtime and service disruptions by implementing redundant components, paths, and failover mechanisms. By leveraging CLI commands to configure redundant physical connectivity, routing protocols, and network services, administrators can design robust and reliable network architectures that meet the demands of mission-critical applications and services and provide continuous access to resources and services for users and customers alike. Failover and disaster recovery strategies for high availability are crucial components of modern IT infrastructure, designed to ensure continuous operation and minimize downtime in the event of hardware failures, software bugs, natural disasters, or other catastrophic events. These strategies involve implementing redundant systems, data replication, and automated failover mechanisms to maintain service availability and data integrity, enabling organizations to meet stringent uptime requirements and business continuity objectives effectively. By deploying failover and disaster recovery strategies using CLI commands, organizations can automate the detection, response, and recovery from outages or disruptions, reducing manual intervention and accelerating recovery times to minimize the impact on users and customers. One of the key techniques in implementing failover and disaster recovery strategies with CLI commands is deploying redundant infrastructure components such as servers, storage devices, and network equipment to eliminate single points of failure and ensure continuous service availability. Administrators can use CLI commands to provision redundant hardware components, configure high-availability clusters, and synchronize data across multiple nodes to maintain consistency and reliability. For example, administrators can use the pacemaker command on Linux servers to configure a high-availability cluster, define resource groups, and specify failover constraints and policies to automate failover and recovery operations, ensuring uninterrupted service availability even if individual nodes or components fail. Additionally, implementing failover and disaster recovery strategies with CLI commands involves configuring data replication and synchronization mechanisms to ensure data consistency and integrity across geographically dispersed locations. Organizations can use CLI commands to configure replication schedules, bandwidth throttling, and conflict resolution policies to replicate data between primary and secondary sites, enabling them to maintain up-to-date copies of critical data and applications and minimize data loss in the event of a disaster or outage. For example, administrators can use the rsync command to synchronize files and directories between servers, specify options such as --delete to remove outdated files, and schedule periodic synchronization tasks using cron jobs or systemd timers to replicate data changes in real-time, ensuring data availability and integrity across distributed environments. Moreover, implementing failover and disaster recovery strategies with CLI commands involves configuring automated failover mechanisms such as virtual IP (VIP) failover, DNS-based failover, or application-level failover to redirect traffic and workload to healthy instances or backup sites in the event of a failure or outage. Administrators can use CLI commands to configure health checks, monitor system status, and trigger failover events based on predefined criteria such as network latency, server load, or application responsiveness, enabling them to maintain service availability and performance even under adverse conditions. For example, administrators can use the ip command on Linux servers to configure a virtual IP address, associate it with multiple network interfaces using the ip addr add command, and use tools such as keepalived or heartbeat to monitor server health and perform failover operations automatically, ensuring continuous access to critical services and applications. Furthermore, implementing failover and disaster *recovery strategies with CLI commands involves testing and validating failover procedures regularly to ensure readiness and effectiveness in real-world scenarios. Organizations can use CLI commands to automate testing procedures, simulate failure scenarios, and measure recovery times to identify potential weaknesses or bottlenecks and refine failover strategies accordingly. For example, administrators can use the curl command to trigger health checks or send test requests to load balancers, monitor response times and error rates, and generate reports or alerts to track performance metrics and validate failover capabilities, enabling them to improve resilience and reliability over time. In summary, implementing failover and disaster recovery strategies with CLI commands is essential for maintaining high availability and resilience in modern IT environments, enabling organizations to minimize downtime, protect data integrity, and meet business continuity objectives effectively. By deploying redundant infrastructure components, configuring data replication and synchronization mechanisms, and automating failover procedures, administrators can ensure continuous service availability and mitigate the impact of outages or disruptions on users and customers, ensuring business operations can continue without interruption.*

Chapter 9: Integrating Hybrid Networking Environments with CLI

Bridging on-premises and cloud networks with CLI commands is a critical aspect of hybrid cloud computing, enabling organizations to establish seamless connectivity and communication between their existing on-premises infrastructure and cloud-based resources and services. This integration allows organizations to leverage the scalability, flexibility, and cost-effectiveness of cloud computing while maintaining connectivity to their legacy systems and applications, facilitating hybrid deployments and enabling gradual migration to the cloud. By deploying bridging solutions using CLI commands, organizations can configure virtual network appliances, VPN connections, and routing policies to bridge the gap between on-premises and cloud environments, enabling secure and efficient data exchange and workload migration. One of the key techniques in bridging on-premises and cloud networks with CLI commands is configuring virtual private network (VPN) connections to establish secure communication tunnels between on-premises data centers or offices and cloud-based virtual networks. Administrators can use CLI commands to provision VPN gateways, configure VPN tunnels, and define routing policies to route traffic between on-premises and cloud networks securely. For example, administrators can use the *az network vnet-gateway create* command in Azure CLI to create a VPN gateway in Azure, specify VPN settings such as gateway type, VPN type, and SKU, and configure connection objects to establish VPN tunnels between on-premises VPN devices and the Azure VPN gateway, enabling secure connectivity and data exchange between on-premises and cloud environments. Additionally, bridging on-premises and cloud networks with CLI commands involves configuring virtual network appliances such as virtual routers, firewalls, or load balancers to act as intermediaries between on-premises and cloud networks, enabling advanced network functions and traffic management capabilities. Administrators can use CLI commands to deploy virtual appliances, configure network interfaces, and define routing policies to route traffic between on-premises and cloud environments efficiently. For example, administrators can use the *gcloud compute instances create* command in Google Cloud CLI to create a virtual machine instance, specify the machine type, boot disk, and network settings, and attach additional network interfaces with custom IP addresses and routing configurations to serve as virtual routers or firewalls, enabling them to implement advanced network functions and policies to bridge on-premises and cloud networks seamlessly. Moreover, bridging on-premises and cloud networks with CLI commands involves configuring routing policies and route propagation mechanisms to enable bidirectional communication and traffic flow between on-premises and cloud environments. Administrators can use CLI commands to configure route tables, route filters, and route propagation settings to advertise on-premises network prefixes to cloud networks and vice versa, enabling seamless connectivity and reachability between distributed environments. For example, administrators can use the aws ec2 create-route command in AWS CLI to create a route in a VPC route table, specify the destination CIDR block and target gateway or virtual appliance, and propagate on-premises routes to the VPC route table using the AWS Direct Connect or VPN gateway, enabling traffic from on-premises networks to reach cloud resources efficiently. Furthermore, bridging on-premises and cloud networks with CLI commands involves implementing network address translation (NAT) and network segmentation techniques to ensure compatibility and security between different network environments. Administrators can use CLI commands to configure NAT gateways, private IP addressing, and network security groups to translate and filter traffic between on-premises and cloud networks, ensuring that only authorized and secure communications are allowed across the bridge. For example, administrators can use the az network public-ip create command in Azure CLI to create a public IP address, associate it with a NAT gateway or load balancer, and configure inbound and outbound NAT rules to translate private IP addresses to public IP addresses and vice versa, enabling secure and transparent communication between on-premises and cloud environments. In summary, bridging on-premises and cloud networks with CLI commands is essential for enabling hybrid cloud deployments, facilitating seamless connectivity and communication between existing on-premises infrastructure and cloud-based resources and services. By configuring VPN connections, deploying virtual network appliances, configuring routing policies, and implementing NAT and network segmentation techniques, administrators can bridge the gap between on-premises and cloud networks effectively, enabling organizations to leverage the benefits of cloud computing while maintaining connectivity to their legacy systems and applications.

Configuring VPNs and ExpressRoute connections is a crucial aspect of networking in cloud environments, enabling organizations to establish secure and reliable connectivity between their on-premises networks and cloud resources. VPNs, or virtual private networks, create encrypted tunnels over the public internet, while ExpressRoute provides private, dedicated connections to Azure. By configuring these connections, organizations can ensure secure data transfer, extend their networks, and enable hybrid cloud architectures. One key technique in configuring VPNs and ExpressRoute connections is setting up VPN gateways or ExpressRoute circuits in the cloud provider's console. In Azure, for instance, administrators can use the az network vpn-gateway create command to create a VPN gateway, specifying parameters such as the gateway type, SKU, and VPN type. Similarly, they can use the az network express-route create command to create an ExpressRoute circuit, providing details like circuit name, peering location, and bandwidth. Once the gateways or circuits are provisioned, organizations can configure the corresponding VPN or ExpressRoute devices on-premises. For VPNs, this involves setting up VPN routers or firewalls and configuring them to establish IPSec tunnels with the cloud VPN gateway. CLI commands like ipsec or crypto are used to configure IPSec parameters such as encryption algorithms, integrity algorithms, and pre-shared keys. With ExpressRoute, organizations need to work with their connectivity provider to set up physical connections and establish BGP (Border Gateway Protocol) sessions for route advertisement. In the Azure portal, administrators can use the az network express-route peering create command to create BGP peerings, specifying parameters such as peering type, peering location, and peer ASN (Autonomous System Number). Additionally, organizations can configure VPN and ExpressRoute connections to support redundancy and failover. For VPNs, this may involve configuring multiple tunnels with dynamic routing protocols like BGP or static routing with IP SLA (Service Level Agreement) monitoring for failover detection.

Administrators can use CLI commands to configure route-based VPNs, enable BGP routing, and set up VPN tunnel monitoring. Similarly, for ExpressRoute, redundant connections can be established by configuring multiple ExpressRoute circuits in different peering locations and using BGP for automatic failover. By utilizing CLI commands, administrators can configure BGP settings, advertise routes, and monitor the health of ExpressRoute connections. Furthermore, organizations can enhance the security of VPNs and ExpressRoute connections by implementing additional authentication mechanisms and encryption protocols. For VPNs, administrators can enable multi-factor authentication (MFA) for VPN users and enforce strong encryption standards like AES-256. They can use CLI commands to configure authentication methods such as RADIUS or LDAP and encryption settings like IKE version and DH group. Similarly, for ExpressRoute, organizations can implement network security controls like access control lists (ACLs) and route filters to restrict traffic and prevent unauthorized access to resources. CLI commands enable administrators to configure security policies, filter rules, and route propagation settings to secure ExpressRoute connections effectively. Additionally, organizations need to monitor and troubleshoot VPNs and ExpressRoute connections to ensure optimal performance and reliability. CLI commands like az network vpn-connection list and az network express-route list provide visibility into the *status and metrics of VPN tunnels and ExpressRoute circuits, allowing administrators to monitor throughput, latency, and packet loss. In case of connectivity issues, administrators can use CLI commands like az network vpn-connection diagnostics or az network express-route troubleshoot to diagnose and troubleshoot VPN and ExpressRoute problems, identify root causes, and implement corrective actions. In summary, configuring VPNs and ExpressRoute connections is essential for establishing secure and reliable connectivity between on-premises networks and cloud resources. By leveraging CLI commands to provision, configure, and manage VPN gateways, ExpressRoute circuits, and associated networking components, organizations can create robust hybrid cloud architectures, enable seamless data transfer, and support mission-critical workloads in the cloud.*

Chapter 10: Optimization Strategies for Network Performance

Fine-tuning network performance with CLI commands is a critical aspect of optimizing the efficiency and reliability of network operations in cloud environments, allowing organizations to achieve better throughput, reduced latency, and improved overall user experience. CLI commands provide administrators with granular control over network configurations, allowing them to adjust parameters, monitor performance metrics, and troubleshoot issues effectively. One key technique in fine-tuning network performance with CLI commands is optimizing network bandwidth allocation and utilization. Administrators can use commands like tc (Traffic Control) on Linux systems to shape and prioritize network traffic, ensuring that critical applications receive adequate bandwidth while less important traffic is throttled or deprioritized. By configuring traffic shaping rules, administrators can enforce Quality of Service (QoS) policies, minimize packet loss, and mitigate congestion, resulting in smoother and more predictable network performance. Additionally, administrators can leverage CLI commands to optimize network protocols and configurations for maximum efficiency. For example, they can use commands like sysctl to adjust kernel parameters related to TCP/IP stack behavior, such as TCP window size, congestion control algorithms, and buffer sizes. By fine-tuning these parameters, administrators can optimize TCP/IP performance, reduce retransmissions, and improve throughput and responsiveness, particularly in high-latency or high-loss network environments. Moreover, CLI commands enable administrators to optimize network routing and path selection to minimize latency and improve reliability. Using commands like ip route or route on Linux systems, administrators can configure static routes, adjust routing metrics, and influence route selection criteria to ensure that traffic takes the most efficient and reliable path between source and destination. By optimizing routing configurations, administrators can reduce latency, avoid network congestion points, and improve overall network performance, particularly for latency-sensitive applications like real-time communications or online gaming. Furthermore, CLI commands facilitate the monitoring and analysis of network performance metrics, allowing administrators to identify bottlenecks, diagnose issues, and fine-tune configurations proactively. Commands like ifconfig, netstat, or ip provide real-time visibility into network interfaces, connections, and traffic statistics, enabling administrators to monitor bandwidth utilization, packet loss, and latency, and identify potential performance issues. Additionally, administrators can use commands like ping or traceroute to perform network diagnostics, measure round-trip times, and trace the path of packets through the network, helping them pinpoint areas of latency or packet loss and take corrective actions to improve performance. Moreover, CLI commands enable administrators to implement advanced network performance monitoring and alerting systems. By leveraging tools like iptables, tcpdump, or Wireshark, administrators can capture and analyze network traffic in real-time, detect anomalies or security threats, and generate alerts or notifications based on predefined criteria. By proactively monitoring network performance and responding to issues promptly, administrators can ensure that the network operates optimally, minimize downtime, and maintain a high level of service availability for users and applications. Additionally, CLI commands allow administrators to fine-tune network security configurations to protect against threats and vulnerabilities while minimizing the impact on performance. Using commands like iptables or firewall-cmd on Linux systems, administrators can configure firewall rules, filter traffic, and enforce security policies to prevent unauthorized access, mitigate denial-of-service (DoS) attacks, and detect and block malicious traffic. By implementing proactive security measures and fine-tuning security configurations, administrators can safeguard network resources and data without compromising performance or usability. In summary, fine-tuning network performance with CLI commands is essential for optimizing the efficiency, reliability, and security of network operations in cloud environments. By leveraging CLI commands to adjust bandwidth allocation, optimize network protocols, configure routing, monitor performance metrics, and enhance security configurations, administrators can ensure that the network meets the requirements of users and applications, delivers consistent performance, and remains resilient to threats and vulnerabilities. Analyzing and optimizing network throughput and latency is crucial for ensuring optimal performance and user experience in cloud environments, as network performance directly impacts the responsiveness and efficiency of applications and services. Administrators can leverage various techniques and CLI commands to measure, analyze, and improve network throughput and latency effectively. One key technique in analyzing network throughput and latency is performing network speed tests using tools like iperf or speedtest-cli. These tools allow administrators to measure the maximum achievable throughput between two endpoints, providing insights into network capacity and performance. By running speed tests between different network segments or locations, administrators can identify bottlenecks, assess network performance variations, and diagnose potential issues affecting throughput and latency. Moreover, administrators can use CLI commands like ping or traceroute to measure network latency and *identify the round-trip time (RTT) between source and destination hosts. By sending ICMP echo requests and analyzing response times, administrators can assess network latency, detect packet loss, and pinpoint areas of network congestion or latency spikes. Additionally, administrators can leverage network monitoring tools like nload or iftop to monitor real-time network traffic and bandwidth utilization. These tools provide visual representations of network traffic patterns, allowing administrators to identify bandwidth-intensive applications, monitor data transfer rates, and detect anomalies or congestion events that may impact network throughput and latency. Furthermore, administrators can optimize network throughput and latency by fine-tuning network configurations and protocols. For example, they can adjust TCP/IP parameters using commands like sysctl or netsh to optimize TCP window size, congestion control algorithms, and buffer sizes for improved performance and efficiency. By optimizing these parameters, administrators can reduce retransmissions, minimize TCP/IP overhead, and maximize throughput while minimizing latency. Additionally, administrators can optimize network routing and path selection to minimize latency and improve reliability using CLI commands like ip route or route. By configuring routing metrics, adjusting route selection criteria, and implementing dynamic routing protocols like BGP or OSPF, administrators can ensure that traffic takes the most efficient and reliable path between source and destination, reducing latency and improving overall network performance. Moreover, administrators can optimize network throughput and latency by implementing Quality of Service (QoS) policies to prioritize traffic and allocate bandwidth based on application requirements. Using CLI commands like tc or qos-policy, administrators can shape and prioritize network traffic, ensuring that critical applications receive sufficient bandwidth and minimizing latency for delay-sensitive applications like voice or video conferencing. Additionally, administrators can implement traffic shaping, rate limiting, and traffic prioritization mechanisms to manage congestion and optimize network performance under varying load conditions. Furthermore, administrators can optimize network throughput and latency by implementing caching and content delivery mechanisms to reduce latency and improve data transfer rates for frequently accessed content. For example, they can deploy caching proxies like Squid or content delivery networks (CDNs) like Cloudflare to cache static content, offload server resources, and reduce latency for end-users. By caching frequently accessed content closer to end-users and optimizing content delivery routes, administrators can improve overall network performance and user experience. In summary, analyzing and optimizing network throughput and latency is essential for ensuring optimal performance, reliability, and user experience in cloud environments.*

By leveraging CLI commands and techniques like network speed tests, latency measurement, real-time traffic monitoring, protocol optimization, routing configuration, QoS implementation, and caching strategies, administrators can identify performance bottlenecks, optimize network configurations, and improve overall network performance, ensuring that applications and services meet the requirements of users and stakeholders.

BOOK 3
ADVANCED AZURE NETWORKING
OPTIMIZING PERFORMANCE AND SECURITY WITH CLI MASTERY

ROB BOTWRIGHT

Chapter 1: Advanced Network Performance Optimization Strategies

Analyzing network performance metrics is vital for maintaining the reliability, efficiency, and security of network infrastructure in cloud environments, as it provides insights into the behavior, usage, and health of network resources. Administrators can leverage various techniques and tools, including CLI commands, to collect, analyze, and interpret network performance metrics effectively. One key technique in analyzing network performance metrics is monitoring network traffic using tools like tcpdump or Wireshark, which capture and analyze packet-level data to provide visibility into network communications and behavior. By capturing and inspecting network packets, administrators can identify traffic patterns, diagnose network issues, and detect anomalies or security threats, helping them optimize network performance and troubleshoot problems efficiently. Moreover, administrators can use CLI commands like netstat or ss to monitor network connections and statistics, providing insights into connection states, bandwidth utilization, and socket-level activity. By analyzing network connection metrics, administrators can identify network congestion, monitor resource usage, and detect potential performance bottlenecks, enabling them to optimize network configurations and improve overall network performance. Additionally, administrators can monitor network bandwidth utilization using tools like nload or iftop, which provide real-time visibility into bandwidth usage and traffic patterns on network interfaces. By monitoring bandwidth utilization, administrators can identify bandwidth-intensive applications, track data transfer rates, and detect network congestion or saturation, enabling them to allocate resources effectively and optimize network performance. Furthermore, administrators can monitor network latency using tools like ping or traceroute, which measure round-trip times (RTT) and trace the path of packets through the network. By monitoring network latency, administrators can identify latency-sensitive applications, diagnose latency issues, and optimize network configurations to reduce latency and improve application responsiveness and user experience. Additionally, administrators can monitor network jitter using tools like mtr or pingplotter, which measure variations in packet delay and provide insights into network stability and reliability. By monitoring network jitter, administrators can detect fluctuations in latency, diagnose network instability, and optimize network configurations to minimize jitter and ensure consistent performance for real-time applications like voice and video conferencing. Moreover, administrators can monitor network errors and packet loss using tools like ifconfig or netstat, which provide visibility into interface error counters and packet loss statistics. By monitoring network errors and packet loss, administrators can identify network issues, diagnose connectivity problems, and troubleshoot network hardware or configuration issues, enabling them to maintain network reliability and performance. Additionally, administrators can analyze network performance metrics using network monitoring and management platforms like Nagios or Zabbix, which provide centralized monitoring, alerting, and reporting capabilities for network infrastructure. By leveraging network monitoring platforms, administrators can collect, visualize, and analyze network performance data from multiple sources, enabling them to identify trends, track performance metrics over time, and proactively detect and address network issues before they impact users or applications. In summary, analyzing network performance metrics is essential for maintaining the reliability, efficiency, and security of network infrastructure in cloud environments. By leveraging CLI commands and tools to monitor network traffic, bandwidth utilization, latency, jitter, errors, and packet loss, administrators can gain insights into network behavior, identify performance issues, and optimize network configurations to ensure optimal performance and user experience. Implementing caching and compression techniques is essential for optimizing the performance, efficiency, and scalability of web applications and services in cloud environments. One key technique in implementing caching is using a reverse proxy server like Nginx or Varnish, which caches static content and serves it directly to clients, reducing server load and improving response times. By configuring caching rules and expiration policies, administrators can control which content is cached and for how long, ensuring that frequently accessed resources are served quickly from cache, reducing latency and improving user experience. Additionally, administrators can use Content Delivery Networks (CDNs) like Cloudflare or Akamai to cache and distribute content across a global network of edge servers, minimizing latency and improving performance for users worldwide. By leveraging CDNs, administrators can offload traffic from origin servers, reduce the impact of spikes in traffic, and ensure consistent performance and availability for users regardless of their location. Furthermore, administrators can implement client-side caching using HTTP headers like Cache-Control and Expires, instructing web browsers to cache resources locally for a specified period. By setting appropriate caching headers, administrators can reduce the number of requests to the server, minimize bandwidth usage, and improve page load times for returning visitors, enhancing the overall performance and scalability of web applications. Moreover, administrators can implement caching at the application level using in-memory caching libraries like Redis or Memcached, which store frequently accessed data in memory for fast retrieval. By caching database queries, API responses, or computed results, administrators can reduce the load on backend databases and application servers, improving scalability and responsiveness, particularly for read-heavy workloads. Additionally, administrators can implement data caching and memoization techniques in application code, storing the results of expensive computations or data transformations for reuse, reducing computational overhead and improving application performance. Furthermore, administrators can implement compression techniques to reduce the size of transmitted data and improve network performance. One key technique in implementing compression is using HTTP compression algorithms like gzip or deflate to compress web content before transmitting it over the network. By enabling compression at the server level, administrators can reduce the amount of data transferred between the server and clients, minimizing bandwidth usage and improving page load times for users. Additionally, administrators can configure web servers like Apache or Nginx to automatically compress web content based on client preferences and capabilities, ensuring compatibility with a wide range of devices and browsers. Moreover, administrators can implement data compression techniques in application code using libraries like zlib or Brotli, compressing data before storage or transmission and decompressing it on the client-side. By compressing JSON responses, XML documents, or binary data, administrators can reduce network latency, improve application performance, and minimize bandwidth usage, particularly for data-intensive web applications or APIs. Furthermore, administrators can implement image compression techniques to optimize the size of images served by web applications, reducing page load times and improving user experience, particularly on mobile devices with limited bandwidth or slower connections. By compressing images using tools like ImageMagick or OptiPNG, administrators can reduce file sizes without sacrificing image quality, ensuring fast and responsive web experiences for users across devices and networks. In summary, implementing caching and compression techniques is essential for optimizing the performance, efficiency, and scalability of web applications and services in cloud environments. By leveraging caching solutions, CDNs, client-side caching, in-memory caching, and compression algorithms, administrators can reduce server load, minimize bandwidth usage, improve page load times, and enhance user experience, ensuring that web applications deliver consistent performance and scalability to users worldwide.

Chapter 2: Fine-Tuning Security Policies with CLI Mastery

Advanced firewall configuration with CLI involves deploying intricate rules and policies to fortify network security, control traffic flow, and mitigate potential threats effectively. One crucial technique is implementing stateful packet inspection using firewalls like iptables or firewalld, which scrutinizes network traffic based on connection state, protocol, and source/destination addresses. By crafting precise firewall rules with commands such as iptables -A INPUT -p tcp --dport 22 -j ACCEPT to permit SSH traffic or firewall-cmd --zone=public --add-service=http --permanent to allow HTTP traffic, administrators can control access to network services and enforce security policies, safeguarding against unauthorized access and malicious activities. Additionally, administrators can configure network address translation (NAT) using CLI commands like iptables -t nat -A POSTROUTING -o eth0 -j MASQUERADE to translate internal IP addresses to external ones, enabling multiple devices within a private network to access the internet using a single public IP address. By implementing NAT, administrators can enhance network security and privacy by hiding internal network topology from external entities while conserving public IP addresses. Furthermore, administrators can deploy application layer firewalls like ModSecurity or Naxsi to inspect and filter HTTP/HTTPS traffic, protecting web applications from common attacks such as SQL injection, cross-site scripting (XSS), and application layer DDoS attacks. By configuring rules to analyze HTTP request parameters and payloads, administrators can detect and block malicious requests, ensuring the integrity and availability of web services. Moreover, administrators can implement network segmentation and zone-based firewalls using tools like iptables or firewalld, dividing the network into distinct security zones and applying different firewall rules to each zone based on trust levels or functional requirements. By creating firewall zones with commands such as firewall-cmd --new-zone=dmz for a demilitarized zone (DMZ) and firewall-cmd --zone=dmz --add-service=http --permanent to allow HTTP traffic, administrators can isolate critical assets and services, minimizing the impact of security breaches and limiting lateral movement by attackers. Additionally, administrators can deploy advanced threat detection and prevention systems like Snort or Suricata to analyze network traffic for suspicious patterns or signatures indicative of known threats or attack techniques. By configuring these systems to monitor network interfaces with commands like suricata -c /etc/suricata/suricata.yaml -i eth0, administrators can detect and block malicious activity in real-time, enhancing network security and incident response capabilities. Furthermore, administrators can implement intrusion detection and prevention systems (IDPS) like Fail2ban or OSSEC to monitor system logs for signs of unauthorized access or suspicious behavior, automatically blocking malicious IP addresses or alerting administrators to potential security incidents. By configuring IDPS rules with commands such as fail2ban-client set sshd banip 192.168.1.100 to ban an IP address after multiple failed SSH login attempts, administrators can proactively defend against brute-force attacks and unauthorized access attempts. Moreover, administrators can leverage threat intelligence feeds and blacklists to enhance firewall protection and block traffic from known malicious sources or IP addresses. By integrating threat feeds with firewalls using tools like ipset or iptables, administrators can automatically update firewall rules to block traffic from malicious IPs or domains, reducing the risk of compromise and enhancing overall network security posture. Additionally, administrators can implement network access control (NAC) solutions like FreeRADIUS or PacketFence to enforce access policies and authenticate users/devices before granting access to the network. By configuring NAC rules with commands such as radiusd -X to start the FreeRADIUS server and pfctl -f /etc/packetfence/pf.conf to apply PacketFence policies, administrators can ensure that only authorized users and devices are allowed to connect to the network, reducing the risk of unauthorized access and insider threats. In summary, advanced *firewall configuration with CLI empowers administrators to strengthen network security, control traffic flow, and protect against a wide range of threats and attacks effectively. By leveraging CLI commands and techniques to deploy stateful packet inspection, NAT, application layer firewalls, network segmentation, threat detection/prevention systems, IDPS, threat intelligence feeds, blacklists, and NAC solutions, administrators can build robust defense mechanisms and fortify their networks against evolving cyber threats and vulnerabilities. Role-Based Access Control (RBAC) best practices are crucial for effectively managing access to resources in complex IT environments, ensuring security, compliance, and efficient resource allocation. One fundamental practice is defining clear roles and responsibilities within the organization, mapping out distinct job functions and the corresponding permissions required to fulfill those roles effectively. By establishing role definitions such as "Administrator," "Developer," and "User," organizations can align access privileges with job requirements, minimizing the risk of over-privileged accounts and unauthorized access. Moreover, organizations should adopt a least privilege principle, granting users the minimum level of access necessary to perform their job functions effectively. This principle mitigates the risk of privilege escalation and limits the potential impact of compromised accounts or insider threats. Administrators can implement RBAC* using tools like Azure CLI to create custom roles with specific permissions tailored to the organization's needs. By defining custom roles with commands such as az role definition create, administrators can enforce granular access controls and align permissions with business requirements accurately. Additionally, organizations should regularly review and update role assignments to reflect changes in job roles, responsibilities, and organizational structure. By conducting periodic access reviews with commands like az role assignment list, administrators can identify and remove unnecessary permissions, ensuring that users have the appropriate level of access at all times. Furthermore, organizations should implement segregation of duties (SoD) controls to prevent conflicts of interest and enforce checks and balances within the organization. By defining role hierarchies and limiting the scope of each role's permissions, organizations can mitigate the risk of fraud, errors, and abuse of privileges. Administrators can enforce SoD controls using RBAC policies and access controls to restrict users from performing conflicting actions or accessing sensitive data. Moreover, organizations should leverage RBAC to enforce separation of environments, ensuring that development, testing, and production environments are isolated and accessed only by authorized personnel. By defining separate roles and permissions for each environment with commands such as az role assignment create, administrators can enforce strict access controls and *prevent unauthorized access or data leakage between environments. Additionally, organizations should implement RBAC for cloud services and applications, aligning access controls with cloud-native security features and compliance standards. By integrating RBAC with cloud identity providers like Azure Active Directory (Azure AD), organizations can centrally manage user identities and access controls across cloud and on-premises environments. Administrators can configure RBAC policies and role assignments using Azure AD groups and user attributes, ensuring consistent access controls and identity management across the organization. Furthermore, organizations should monitor and audit RBAC activities to detect and respond to unauthorized access attempts or policy violations promptly. By enabling RBAC logging and auditing with commands like az monitor diagnostic-settings create, administrators can capture detailed logs of role assignments, permissions changes, and access attempts for analysis and review. Moreover, organizations should leverage RBAC to enforce compliance with regulatory requirements and industry standards, such as GDPR, HIPAA, and PCI DSS. By aligning RBAC policies with compliance frameworks and implementing controls to enforce data privacy, confidentiality, and integrity, organizations can demonstrate adherence to regulatory requirements and protect sensitive information effectively. In summary, Role-Based Access Control (RBAC) best practices are essential for organizations to manage access to resources securely, comply with regulatory requirements, and maintain efficient operations. By defining clear roles and responsibilities, adopting a least privilege principle, regularly reviewing and updating role assignments, implementing segregation of duties (SoD) controls, enforcing separation of environments, integrating RBAC with cloud services and applications, monitoring and auditing RBAC activities, and ensuring compliance with regulatory requirements, organizations can strengthen their security posture and protect against unauthorized access, data breaches, and compliance violations effectively.*

Chapter 3: Implementing Advanced Network Traffic Management Techniques

Quality of Service (QoS) configuration with CLI is essential for optimizing network performance, ensuring reliable service delivery, and prioritizing critical traffic types over less important ones. One fundamental aspect of QoS configuration is traffic classification, where network traffic is categorized based on predefined criteria such as source/destination IP addresses, port numbers, or protocol types. Administrators can use CLI commands like tc filter add to classify traffic and assign it to specific traffic classes or queues based on its characteristics. By creating traffic classification rules with commands such as tc filter add dev eth0 protocol ip parent 1:0 prio 1 u32 match ip dst 192.168.1.0/24 flowid 1:10 to classify traffic destined for a specific IP subnet and assign it to a priority queue, administrators can ensure that critical traffic receives preferential treatment and sufficient bandwidth. Moreover, administrators can configure traffic shaping and bandwidth management to control the rate of data transmission and prevent network congestion. With CLI commands like tc qdisc add dev eth0 root tbf rate 1mbit burst 32kbit latency 50ms, administrators can enforce rate limits on outgoing traffic from a network interface, ensuring that it conforms to specified bandwidth constraints and preventing it from exceeding predefined thresholds. Additionally, administrators can prioritize traffic using techniques such as packet marking and Differentiated Services Code Point (DSCP) tagging to signal the importance of packets to network devices and routers. By marking packets with specific DSCP values using commands like iptables -t mangle -A POSTROUTING -p tcp --dport 80 -j DSCP --set-dscp 46, administrators can prioritize traffic such as HTTP traffic over less critical traffic types, ensuring that it receives preferential treatment during periods of congestion. Furthermore, administrators can implement traffic policing and rate limiting to enforce bandwidth quotas and prevent individual users or applications from monopolizing network resources. With CLI commands like tc qdisc add dev eth0 root handle 1: cbq avpkt 1000 bandwidth 10mbit, administrators can create a class-based queuing (CBQ) discipline to allocate bandwidth fairly among different traffic classes and enforce rate limits on each class to prevent excessive bandwidth consumption. Additionally, administrators can deploy traffic prioritization techniques such as Weighted Fair Queuing (WFQ) or Hierarchical Token Bucket (HTB) to ensure equitable resource allocation and prevent low-priority traffic from starving high-priority traffic of bandwidth. By configuring queuing disciplines with commands like tc qdisc add dev eth0 root handle 1: htb default 10, administrators can organize traffic into hierarchical queues and assign each queue a specific share of available bandwidth, allowing critical traffic to bypass queues with lower priority traffic and receive expedited treatment. Moreover, administrators can implement congestion avoidance mechanisms such as Random Early Detection (RED) or Explicit Congestion Notification (ECN) to proactively manage network congestion and prevent packet loss. With CLI commands like tc qdisc add dev eth0 root handle 1: red min 30000 max 60000 avpkt 1000 burst 20 probability 0.02 ecn, administrators can configure RED to monitor packet queue lengths and selectively drop packets before congestion becomes severe, allowing TCP congestion control mechanisms to react appropriately and maintain network stability. Additionally, administrators can use ECN to notify endpoints of impending congestion and request reduced transmission rates, enabling them to adjust their sending rates proactively and mitigate congestion without resorting to packet loss. Furthermore, administrators can implement QoS policies to prioritize latency-sensitive applications such as voice over IP (VoIP) or video conferencing, ensuring that they receive sufficient bandwidth and low latency to maintain quality performance. By configuring QoS policies with commands like tc filter add dev eth0 protocol udp parent 1:0 prio 1 u32 match ip dport 5060 0xffff flowid 1:10, administrators can identify and prioritize VoIP traffic based on its destination port number and assign it to a high-priority queue, *guaranteeing that it receives timely delivery and minimal delay. In summary, Quality of Service (QoS) configuration with CLI is essential for optimizing network performance, ensuring reliable service delivery, and prioritizing critical traffic types over less important ones. By employing traffic classification, traffic shaping, bandwidth management, traffic prioritization, traffic policing, rate limiting, congestion avoidance, and QoS policies, administrators can effectively manage network resources, meet service level agreements (SLAs), and deliver a consistent and high-quality user experience.*

Traffic shaping and prioritization strategies are essential components of network management, allowing administrators to optimize bandwidth utilization, prioritize critical applications, and ensure a consistent user experience. One fundamental technique in traffic shaping is the use of traffic policing, which involves enforcing bandwidth limits on specific types of traffic to prevent network congestion and ensure fair resource allocation. Administrators can deploy traffic policing using commands like tc qdisc add dev eth0 root tbf rate 1mbit burst 32kbit latency 50ms, which configures a token bucket filter (TBF) to limit the rate of outgoing traffic on a network interface to 1 megabit per second, with a burst size of 32 kilobits and a latency of 50 milliseconds. Moreover, administrators can implement traffic shaping policies to prioritize certain types of traffic over others, ensuring that critical applications receive sufficient bandwidth and low latency to maintain performance. By configuring traffic shaping policies with commands like tc qdisc add dev eth0 root handle 1: htb default 10, administrators can organize traffic into hierarchical queues and assign each queue a specific share of available bandwidth, allowing them to prioritize critical applications and allocate resources based on their importance. Additionally, administrators can leverage Quality of Service (QoS) mechanisms such as Differentiated Services Code Point (DSCP) tagging to mark packets with specific priorities and ensure that they receive preferential treatment throughout the network. With commands like iptables -t mangle -A POSTROUTING -p tcp --dport 80 -j DSCP --set-dscp 46, administrators can mark packets destined for specific ports, such as port 80 for HTTP traffic, with a DSCP value of 46, indicating that they should receive expedited forwarding and minimal delay. Furthermore, administrators can implement traffic prioritization at the application level, using techniques such as Class-Based Queuing (CBQ) to allocate bandwidth based on application requirements and user priorities. By defining traffic classes and assigning them specific bandwidth allocations with commands like tc qdisc add dev eth0 root handle 1: cbq avpkt 1000 bandwidth 10mbit, administrators can ensure that critical applications receive sufficient bandwidth to meet their performance requirements, while less important applications are limited to prevent them from monopolizing network resources.

Moreover, administrators can deploy traffic shaping and prioritization strategies to optimize network performance for specific use cases, such as voice over IP (VoIP) or video conferencing, where low latency and consistent bandwidth are critical for quality communication. By prioritizing VoIP traffic with commands like tc filter add dev eth0 protocol udp parent 1:0 prio 1 u32 match ip dport 5060 0xffff flowid 1:10, administrators can ensure that VoIP packets receive expedited treatment and minimal delay, enabling clear and uninterrupted voice communication. Additionally, administrators can implement traffic shaping policies to control the flow of data between different network segments and prevent congestion at critical points in the network. With commands like tc filter add dev eth0 parent 1:0 protocol ip prio 1 u32 match ip dst 192.168.1.0/24 flowid 1:10, administrators can classify traffic based on destination IP addresses and assign it to specific queues, allowing them to manage bandwidth usage and optimize performance for different network segments. Furthermore, administrators can monitor network traffic and performance metrics to identify bottlenecks and fine-tune traffic shaping policies accordingly. By analyzing traffic patterns and utilization data with tools like iftop and nload, administrators can gain insights into network behavior and adjust traffic shaping parameters to optimize performance and ensure a consistent user experience. In summary, traffic shaping and *prioritization strategies are essential for optimizing network performance, ensuring fair resource allocation, and maintaining a consistent user experience. By implementing traffic policing, traffic shaping policies, QoS mechanisms, application-level prioritization, and monitoring tools, administrators can effectively manage network traffic, prioritize critical applications, and optimize performance for specific use cases, enabling organizations to meet their business objectives and deliver reliable services to end users.*

Chapter 4: Enhancing Network Resilience with CLI Tools

Implementing redundancy and failover solutions is crucial for ensuring high availability and reliability in network infrastructure. One fundamental technique in achieving redundancy is through the use of redundant hardware components such as network interfaces, switches, and routers. Administrators can deploy redundancy at the hardware level by configuring devices in a redundant configuration, such as setting up network interfaces in a bonded configuration using the ifenslave command on Linux systems. This command allows administrators to combine multiple network interfaces into a single logical interface, providing redundancy and load balancing across multiple physical links. Additionally, administrators can implement redundancy at the network level by deploying redundant network paths and devices to ensure continuous connectivity in the event of a failure. This can be achieved using protocols such as Spanning Tree Protocol (STP) or Rapid Spanning Tree Protocol (RSTP), which dynamically manage network topology and prevent loops by blocking redundant paths. With commands like spanning-tree vlan 1 priority 4096 on Cisco switches, administrators can configure STP parameters to prioritize certain switches as root bridges and optimize network convergence.

Moreover, administrators can leverage Virtual Router Redundancy Protocol (VRRP) or its variants, such as Hot Standby Router Protocol (HSRP) or Virtual Router Redundancy Protocol version 3 (VRRPv3), to provide redundancy for routers and gateway devices. By configuring VRRP groups with commands like vrrp 1 ip 192.168.1.1, administrators can assign a virtual IP address to a group of routers and ensure seamless failover in the event of a primary router failure. Furthermore, administrators can deploy redundant network connections and links using techniques such as link aggregation or multipath routing to improve network reliability and performance. By configuring link aggregation groups (LAGs) with commands like interface port-channel 1, administrators can bundle multiple physical links into a single logical link, providing redundancy and increased bandwidth capacity. Additionally, administrators can implement multipath routing protocols such as Equal-Cost Multipath (ECMP) or Multipath TCP (MPTCP) to distribute traffic across multiple network paths and ensure fault tolerance. With commands like ip route add default nexthop via 192.168.1.1 dev eth0, administrators can configure routing tables to include multiple next-hop addresses and enable ECMP routing for load balancing and redundancy. Moreover, administrators can deploy redundant network services and applications using techniques such as clustering or load balancing to ensure continuous operation and fault tolerance. By setting up clustered services with tools like Pacemaker and Corosync on Linux systems, administrators can create redundant configurations for critical services such as DNS, DHCP, or web servers, ensuring high availability and automatic failover in the event of a node failure. Additionally, administrators can implement load balancing solutions using tools like HAProxy or Nginx to distribute incoming traffic across multiple backend servers, providing redundancy and scalability for web applications and services. With commands like proxy_pass http://backend_servers; in Nginx configuration files, administrators can configure reverse proxying and load balancing to distribute incoming HTTP requests across a pool of backend servers. Furthermore, administrators can leverage cloud-based redundancy and failover solutions such as Amazon Web Services (AWS) Elastic Load Balancing (ELB) or Azure Traffic Manager to achieve high availability and fault tolerance for applications and services deployed in the cloud. By configuring load balancers with features like health checks and automatic failover, administrators can ensure continuous availability and reliability for cloud-based applications and services, even in the event of infrastructure failures or outages. In summary, implementing redundancy and failover solutions is essential for ensuring high availability, reliability, and fault tolerance in network infrastructure. By deploying redundant hardware components, network paths, devices, connections, services, and applications, *administrators can minimize downtime, mitigate the impact of failures, and maintain uninterrupted operation for critical systems and services. Disaster recovery planning for network outages is a critical aspect of ensuring business continuity and minimizing downtime in the event of unforeseen disruptions. One fundamental technique in disaster recovery planning is the creation of comprehensive backup and recovery strategies to safeguard critical network infrastructure and data. Administrators can deploy backup solutions such as Veeam Backup & Replication or Backup Exec to create regular backups of network configurations, device configurations, and data, ensuring that they can quickly restore operations in the event of a network outage. By scheduling automated backups with commands like veeamconfig job create --name "Daily Backup" --type backup --object "Entire Infrastructure" --schedule "Daily at 2:00 AM", administrators can ensure that critical network components are backed up regularly and reliably, minimizing the risk of data loss and downtime. Moreover, administrators can implement redundant network connections and paths to ensure continuous connectivity and availability in the event of a network outage. This can be achieved by deploying redundant network links, routers, switches, and Internet Service Providers (ISPs) to provide multiple paths for traffic to reach its destination. With commands like ip route add default nexthop via 192.168.1.2 dev eth1, administrators can configure* routing tables to include redundant next-hop addresses, enabling automatic failover and route redundancy in case of link failure. Additionally, administrators can leverage cloud-based disaster recovery solutions such as Azure Site Recovery or AWS Disaster Recovery to replicate critical network infrastructure and data to the cloud, providing a resilient and scalable backup solution for disaster recovery. By configuring replication policies with commands like az backup protection enable-for-vm -- vm "MyVM" --policy-name "DailyReplication", administrators can replicate virtual machines and data to the cloud at regular intervals, ensuring that they have a copy of their network infrastructure and data readily available for recovery in case of an outage. Furthermore, administrators can implement failover and failback procedures to quickly restore operations and minimize downtime in the event of a network outage. By creating failover plans and runbooks with tools like Azure Automation or Ansible, administrators can automate the process of migrating workloads, applications, and data to redundant or backup infrastructure in the event of a failure, ensuring seamless continuity of operations. With commands like az network traffic-manager endpoint set-status --name "MyEndpoint" --profile-name "MyTrafficManagerProfile" --resource-group "MyResourceGroup" --status Disabled, administrators can disable traffic endpoints and reroute traffic to redundant or backup systems during a network *outage, minimizing disruption to users and services. Additionally, administrators can conduct regular disaster recovery drills and exercises to test the effectiveness of their plans and procedures and identify any weaknesses or areas for improvement. By simulating network outages and practicing failover and failback procedures with tools like VMware vSphere Site Recovery Manager or Microsoft Hyper-V Replica, administrators can validate their disaster recovery plans and ensure that they are prepared to respond effectively to real-world incidents.*

Chapter 5: Advanced Network Troubleshooting and Diagnostics

Utilizing packet captures and protocol analysis is essential for network administrators to diagnose and troubleshoot network issues effectively. Packet captures, also known as network sniffing or packet sniffing, involve capturing and analyzing the data packets flowing through a network interface in real-time or from a previously captured file. One widely used tool for packet capture and analysis is Wireshark, a free and open-source network protocol analyzer. With Wireshark, administrators can capture packets on specific network interfaces or from specific IP addresses and analyze them to identify network anomalies, performance issues, or security threats. The command wireshark -i eth0 initiates packet capture on the Ethernet interface eth0, allowing administrators to monitor network traffic in real-time. Additionally, Wireshark provides powerful filtering capabilities, allowing administrators to focus on specific protocols, conversations, or packet types, making it easier to pinpoint the source of network problems. By applying display filters such as ip.addr == 192.168.1.1 or tcp.port == 80, administrators can narrow down the captured packets to those relevant to specific IP addresses or TCP ports, facilitating efficient analysis and troubleshooting. Furthermore, protocol analysis involves examining the structure and behavior of network protocols to understand how data is transmitted, received, and processed across a network. Tools like tcpdump and tshark, command-line packet analyzers similar to Wireshark, enable administrators to capture and analyze network traffic directly from the command line. With tcpdump, administrators can capture packets on specific network interfaces or with specific filter criteria, such as tcpdump -i eth0 to capture packets on interface eth0 or tcpdump host 192.168.1.1 to capture packets involving host 192.168.1.1. Similarly, tshark provides command-line access to Wireshark's packet analysis capabilities, allowing administrators to perform protocol analysis directly from the terminal. By running commands like tshark -i eth0 -Y "ip.addr == 192.168.1.1", administrators can capture and filter packets based on specific criteria, making it easier to identify and troubleshoot network issues. Moreover, protocol analysis tools enable administrators to inspect packet headers, payload contents, and protocol-specific fields to identify abnormalities, errors, or misconfigurations in network communications. By examining protocol headers such as IP, TCP, UDP, and ICMP, administrators can identify issues such as packet loss, latency, retransmissions, or malformed packets that may indicate underlying network problems. Additionally, protocol analysis tools provide statistical information and graphical representations of network traffic patterns, allowing administrators to visualize and analyze network behavior over time. This can help identify trends, anomalies, or performance bottlenecks that may require further investigation or optimization. Furthermore, packet captures and protocol analysis play a crucial role in network security by enabling administrators to detect and investigate suspicious or malicious network activity. By analyzing packet contents, flow patterns, and communication behavior, administrators can identify potential security threats such as malware infections, unauthorized access attempts, or data exfiltration attempts. Additionally, protocol analysis tools can help administrators monitor compliance with network security policies, identify vulnerabilities, and assess the effectiveness of security controls and countermeasures. Overall, utilizing packet captures and protocol analysis is essential for maintaining network performance, reliability, and security in modern IT environments. By leveraging the capabilities of tools like Wireshark, tcpdump, and tshark, administrators can gain valuable insights into network behavior, diagnose problems efficiently, and ensure the integrity and availability of critical network infrastructure.

Advanced troubleshooting techniques with CLI tools are essential for network administrators to effectively diagnose and resolve complex issues that may arise in networking environments. One powerful CLI tool for network troubleshooting is the ping command, which is used to test the reachability of a host on an IP network and measure the round-trip time for packets sent to that host. By executing the ping command followed by the IP address or hostname of the target host, administrators can quickly determine whether the host is reachable and assess network latency and packet loss. Additionally, the traceroute command is another valuable tool for diagnosing network connectivity issues by displaying the route that packets take to reach a destination host. By executing the traceroute command followed by the IP address or hostname of the target host, administrators can identify intermediate routers or network devices along the path to the destination, helping pinpoint potential points of failure or congestion. Furthermore, the netstat command provides administrators with detailed information about network connections, routing tables, interface statistics, and multicast group memberships on a system. By running the netstat command with appropriate options such as -t for TCP connections or -u for UDP connections, administrators can troubleshoot issues related to network services, connection states, and resource utilization, helping identify and resolve network bottlenecks or performance problems. Moreover, the tcpdump command is a powerful packet analyzer that allows administrators to capture and analyze network traffic in real-time or from a previously captured file. By running the tcpdump command with filters such as -i for specifying the network interface or -s for limiting the packet size, administrators can capture packets relevant to specific network traffic patterns or protocols, facilitating efficient troubleshooting and analysis. Additionally, the ip command, part of the iproute2 suite of utilities, provides administrators with extensive capabilities for configuring and managing network interfaces, routing tables, and network namespaces on Linux systems. By using subcommands such as ip addr for managing IP addresses, ip route for managing routing tables, and ip link for managing network interfaces, administrators can perform advanced network troubleshooting tasks such as interface configuration, route manipulation, and traffic filtering, helping resolve connectivity issues and optimize network performance. Furthermore, the nslookup command is a useful tool for troubleshooting DNS-related issues by querying DNS servers to resolve domain names to IP addresses and vice versa. By executing the nslookup command followed by the hostname or IP address of the target host, administrators can verify DNS resolution, troubleshoot DNS server connectivity problems, and diagnose DNS configuration issues, ensuring reliable name resolution in the network environment. Additionally, the iftop command is a command-line tool for monitoring network bandwidth usage in real-time by displaying a list of network connections and their corresponding bandwidth usage. By running the iftop command with options such as -i for specifying the network interface or -B for displaying traffic in bytes instead of bits, *administrators can identify bandwidth-intensive applications or users, troubleshoot network congestion issues, and optimize network performance. Moreover, the ss command is another useful tool for displaying detailed information about network sockets, connections, and statistics on a system. By running the ss command with options such as -t for TCP sockets or -u for UDP sockets, administrators can analyze network activity, monitor connection states, and diagnose issues related to network services or protocols, aiding in troubleshooting and resolution. Additionally, the arp command is a utility for viewing and modifying the Address Resolution Protocol (ARP) cache, which maps IP addresses to MAC addresses on a local network. By executing the arp command with options such as -a for displaying the ARP cache or -d for deleting ARP entries, administrators can troubleshoot ARP-related issues such as IP conflicts or incorrect mappings, ensuring proper communication between devices on the network. Furthermore, the iptables command is a powerful firewall utility for configuring packet filtering, network address translation (NAT), and packet mangling rules on Linux systems. By using the iptables command with options such as -A for appending rules or -D for deleting rules, administrators can control network traffic, enforce security policies, and mitigate threats or attacks, enhancing the security posture of the network environment. Additionally, the iptraf command is a console-based network monitoring utility that provides administrators with real-time statistics for various network interfaces, connections, and protocols. By running the iptraf command with options such as -i for specifying the network interface or -s for displaying summary statistics, administrators can monitor network traffic, identify performance bottlenecks, and troubleshoot issues related to network utilization or congestion, helping optimize network performance and reliability. Moreover, the mtr command, short for My TraceRoute, is a network diagnostic tool that combines the functionality of ping and traceroute to provide comprehensive information about network connectivity and performance to a destination host. By executing the mtr command followed by the hostname or IP address of the target host, administrators can perform continuous traceroute and ping tests, analyze network latency and packet loss, and identify network issues affecting connectivity or performance, facilitating efficient troubleshooting and resolution. Additionally, the nmap command is a versatile network scanning tool for discovering hosts and services on a network, assessing network security, and identifying potential vulnerabilities or misconfigurations. By running the nmap command with options such as -sS for TCP SYN scan or -sU for UDP scan, administrators can perform comprehensive network scans, detect open ports, and enumerate network services, aiding in vulnerability assessment and risk mitigation. Furthermore, the sshd command is a secure shell daemon that provides* encrypted remote access to a system over a network, allowing administrators to securely manage and troubleshoot remote systems. By starting the sshd service and configuring SSH access control settings, administrators can establish secure remote connections, execute commands remotely, and troubleshoot issues on remote systems, enhancing operational efficiency and flexibility. Additionally, the ipconfig command is a utility for viewing and configuring network interface settings, such as IP address, subnet mask, and default gateway, on Windows systems. By executing the ipconfig command with options such as /all for displaying detailed information or /release and /renew for releasing and renewing DHCP leases, administrators can troubleshoot network connectivity issues, renew IP configurations, and diagnose DHCP-related problems, ensuring reliable network communication on Windows-based networks. Moreover, the netsh command is a command-line scripting utility for managing network settings, interfaces, and services on Windows systems. By running the netsh command with subcommands such as netsh interface ipv4 show addresses for displaying IP configurations or netsh firewall show config for viewing firewall settings, administrators can troubleshoot network issues, configure network parameters, and manage network security policies, aiding in network optimization and security enforcement. Additionally, the tcpdump command is a packet analyzer that allows *administrators to capture and analyze network traffic in real-time or from a previously captured file on Unix-like systems. By running the tcpdump command with options such as -i for specifying the network interface or -s for limiting the packet size, administrators can capture packets relevant to specific network traffic patterns or protocols, facilitating efficient troubleshooting and analysis. Moreover, the ss command is a powerful tool for displaying detailed information about network sockets, connections, and statistics on a system. By executing the ss command with options such as -t for TCP sockets or -u for UDP sockets, administrators can analyze network activity, monitor connection states, and diagnose issues related to network services or protocols, aiding in troubleshooting and resolution. Additionally, the arp command is a utility for viewing and modifying the Address Resolution Protocol (ARP) cache, which maps IP addresses to MAC addresses on a local network. By executing the arp command with options such as -a for displaying the ARP cache or -d for deleting ARP entries, administrators can troubleshoot ARP-related issues such as IP conflicts or incorrect mappings, ensuring proper communication between devices on the network. Furthermore, the iptables command is a powerful firewall utility for configuring packet filtering, network address translation (NAT), and packet mangling rules on Linux systems. By using the iptables command with options such as -A for appending rules or -D for deleting rules, administrators can control network traffic, enforce security policies, and mitigate threats or attacks, enhancing the security posture of the network environment. Additionally, the iptraf command is a console-based network monitoring utility that provides administrators with real-time statistics for various network interfaces, connections, and protocols. By running the iptraf command with options such as -i for specifying the network interface or -s for displaying summary statistics, administrators can monitor network traffic, identify performance bottlenecks, and troubleshoot issues related to network utilization or congestion, helping optimize network performance and reliability. Moreover, the mtr command, short for My TraceRoute, is a network diagnostic tool that combines the functionality of ping and traceroute to provide comprehensive information about network connectivity and performance to a destination host. By executing the mtr command followed by the hostname or IP address of the target host, administrators can perform continuous traceroute and ping tests, analyze network latency and packet loss, and identify network issues affecting connectivity or performance, facilitating efficient troubleshooting and resolution. Additionally, the nmap command is a versatile network scanning tool for discovering hosts and services on a network, assessing network security, and identifying potential vulnerabilities or misconfigurations. By running the nmap command with options such as -sS for TCP SYN* scan or -sU for UDP scan, administrators can perform comprehensive network scans, detect open ports, and enumerate network services, aiding in vulnerability assessment and risk mitigation. Furthermore, the sshd command is a secure shell daemon that provides encrypted remote access to a system over a network, allowing administrators to securely manage and troubleshoot remote systems. By starting the sshd service and configuring SSH access control settings, administrators can establish secure remote connections, execute commands remotely, and troubleshoot issues on remote systems, enhancing operational efficiency and flexibility. Additionally, the ipconfig command is a utility for viewing and configuring network interface settings, such as IP address, subnet mask, and default gateway, on Windows systems. By executing the ipconfig command with options such as /all for displaying detailed information or /release and /renew for releasing and renewing DHCP leases, administrators can troubleshoot network connectivity issues, renew IP configurations, and diagnose DHCP-related problems, ensuring reliable network communication on Windows-based networks. Moreover, the netsh command is a command-line scripting utility for managing network settings, interfaces, and services on Windows systems. By running the netsh command with subcommands such as netsh interface ipv4 show addresses for displaying IP configurations or netsh firewall show config for viewing firewall settings, *administrators can troubleshoot network issues, configure network parameters, and manage network security policies, aiding in network optimization and security enforcement. Additionally, the tcpdump command is a packet analyzer that allows administrators to capture and analyze network traffic in real-time or from a previously captured file on Unix-like systems. By running the tcpdump command with options such as -i for specifying the network interface or -s for limiting the packet size, administrators can capture packets relevant to specific network traffic patterns or protocols, facilitating efficient troubleshooting and analysis. Moreover, the ss command is a powerful tool for displaying detailed information about network sockets, connections, and statistics on a system. By executing the ss command with options such as -t for TCP sockets or -u for UDP sockets, administrators can analyze network activity, monitor connection states, and diagnose issues related to network services or protocols, aiding in troubleshooting and resolution. Additionally, the arp command is a utility for viewing and modifying the Address Resolution Protocol (ARP) cache, which maps IP addresses to MAC addresses on a local network. By executing the arp command with options such as -a for displaying the ARP cache or -d for deleting ARP entries, administrators can troubleshoot ARP-related issues such as IP conflicts or incorrect mappings, ensuring proper communication between devices on the network. Furthermore, the iptables command is a* powerful firewall utility for configuring packet filtering, network address translation (NAT), and packet mangling rules on Linux systems. By using the iptables command with options such as -A for appending rules or -D for deleting rules, administrators can control network traffic, enforce security policies, and mitigate threats or attacks, enhancing the security posture of the network environment. Additionally, the iptraf command is a console-based network monitoring utility that provides administrators with real-time statistics for various network interfaces, connections, and protocols. By running the iptraf command with options such as -i for specifying the network interface or -s for displaying summary statistics, administrators can monitor network traffic, identify performance bottlenecks, and troubleshoot issues related to network utilization or congestion, helping optimize network performance and reliability. Moreover, the mtr command, short for My TraceRoute, is a network diagnostic tool that combines the functionality of ping and traceroute to provide comprehensive information about network connectivity and performance to a destination host. By executing the mtr command followed by the hostname or IP address of the target host, administrators can perform continuous traceroute and ping tests, analyze network latency and packet loss, and identify network issues affecting connectivity or performance, facilitating efficient troubleshooting and resolution. Additionally, the *nmap command is a versatile network scanning tool for discovering hosts and services on a network, assessing network security, and identifying potential vulnerabilities or misconfigurations. By running the nmap command with options such as -sS for TCP SYN scan or -sU for UDP scan, administrators can perform comprehensive network scans, detect open ports, and enumerate network services, aiding in vulnerability assessment and risk mitigation. Furthermore, the sshd command is a secure shell daemon that provides encrypted remote access to a system over a network, allowing administrators to securely manage and troubleshoot remote systems. By starting the sshd service and configuring SSH access control settings, administrators can establish secure remote connections, execute commands remotely, and troubleshoot issues on remote systems, enhancing operational efficiency and flexibility. Additionally, the ipconfig command is a utility for viewing and configuring network interface settings, such as IP address, subnet mask, and default gateway, on Windows systems. By executing the ipconfig command with options such as /all for displaying detailed information or /release and /renew for releasing and renewing DHCP leases, administrators can troubleshoot network connectivity issues, renew IP configurations, and diagnose DHCP-related problems, ensuring reliable network communication on Windows-based networks. Moreover, the netsh command is a command-line scripting utility for* managing network settings, interfaces, and services on Windows systems. By running the netsh command with subcommands such as netsh interface ipv4 show addresses for displaying IP configurations or netsh firewall show config for viewing firewall settings, administrators can troubleshoot network issues, configure network parameters, and manage network security policies, aiding in network optimization and security enforcement. Additionally, the tcpdump command is a packet analyzer that allows administrators to capture and analyze network traffic in real-time or from a previously captured file on Unix-like systems. By running the tcpdump command with options such as -i for specifying the network interface or -s for limiting the packet size, administrators can capture packets relevant to specific network traffic patterns or protocols, facilitating efficient troubleshooting and analysis. Moreover, the ss command is a powerful tool for displaying detailed information about network sockets, connections, and statistics on a system. By executing the ss command with options such as -t for TCP sockets or -u for UDP sockets, administrators can analyze network activity, monitor connection states, and diagnose issues related to network services or protocols, aiding in troubleshooting and resolution. Additionally, the arp command is a utility for viewing and modifying the Address Resolution Protocol (ARP) cache, which maps IP addresses to MAC addresses on a local network. By executing the arp command with options such as -a *for displaying the ARP cache or -d for deleting ARP entries, administrators can troubleshoot ARP-related issues such as IP conflicts or incorrect mappings, ensuring proper communication between devices on the network. Furthermore, the iptables command is a powerful firewall utility for configuring packet filtering, network address translation (NAT), and packet mangling rules on Linux systems. By using the iptables command with options such as -A for appending rules or -D for deleting rules, administrators can control network traffic, enforce security policies, and mitigate threats or attacks, enhancing the security posture of the network environment.*

Chapter 6: Implementing Secure Connectivity Solutions

Secure tunneling and VPN configuration with CLI tools are fundamental aspects of network security and remote access management. One powerful CLI command for setting up a VPN tunnel is openvpn, which is widely used for creating secure connections between devices over untrusted networks. By running the openvpn command followed by the configuration file, administrators can establish encrypted VPN tunnels using the OpenVPN protocol, ensuring data confidentiality and integrity across the network. Additionally, the ipsec command is another essential tool for configuring IPsec-based VPNs, which provide strong encryption and authentication for network communications. By using the ipsec command with subcommands such as ipsec tunnel and ipsec policy, administrators can define VPN tunnels, specify encryption algorithms, and configure security policies to protect data transmission between endpoints. Moreover, the ssh command can be utilized for creating secure tunnels, also known as SSH tunnels or port forwarding, to encrypt and forward network traffic between local and remote hosts. By executing the ssh command with options such as -L for local port forwarding or -R for remote port forwarding, administrators can establish encrypted tunnels for accessing remote services securely or bypassing network restrictions, enhancing data privacy and accessibility. Furthermore, the stunnel command is a lightweight SSL encryption wrapper that can be used to secure communication channels between applications or network services. By configuring the stunnel service with a custom configuration file specifying the SSL certificate and desired encryption settings, administrators can encrypt and decrypt traffic between endpoints transparently, protecting sensitive data from eavesdropping or tampering. Additionally, the ip command, part of the iproute2 suite of utilities, can be employed for configuring network interfaces, routing tables, and IPsec policies to support VPN deployments. By using subcommands such as ip tunnel for creating IP tunnels or ip xfrm for managing IPsec policies, administrators can customize VPN configurations to meet specific security and connectivity requirements, ensuring robust protection and seamless connectivity across the network. Moreover, the strongswan command is a versatile VPN solution that supports various VPN protocols, including IPsec and IKEv2, for establishing secure tunnels between devices. By configuring the strongswan service with a custom configuration file and deploying appropriate IPsec policies, administrators can deploy scalable VPN solutions with advanced features such as multi-site connectivity, certificate-based authentication, and dynamic routing, ensuring secure and reliable communication across distributed networks. Additionally, the wireguard command is a modern VPN protocol that offers high-performance, secure tunneling capabilities with minimal overhead. By installing the WireGuard kernel module and configuring the wireguard service with peer-to-peer connections and encryption keys, administrators can deploy lightweight and efficient VPN solutions for secure communication between devices, enhancing network privacy and performance. Furthermore, the openconnect command is a client for connecting to Cisco AnyConnect VPN servers, which are widely used in enterprise environments for remote access and secure connectivity. By running the openconnect command with options such as -u for specifying the username or -b for running in the background, administrators can establish encrypted VPN connections to Cisco AnyConnect servers, enabling authorized users to access corporate resources securely from remote locations. Additionally, the softether-vpnserver command is a comprehensive VPN server solution that supports multiple VPN protocols, including SSL VPN, L2TP/IPsec, and SSTP, for flexible and secure remote access. By configuring the SoftEther VPN server with user accounts, authentication methods, and access control policies, administrators can deploy robust VPN infrastructures to accommodate diverse client devices and connectivity requirements, ensuring secure communication and data protection across the network. Moreover, the openvpn-as command is a convenient VPN server solution that provides a web-based administration interface for managing VPN users, configurations, and access control settings. By installing and configuring the OpenVPN Access Server with the openvpn-as command, administrators can quickly deploy scalable VPN solutions with user-friendly management capabilities, simplifying the setup and administration of VPN services for remote users and devices. Additionally, the strongswan command is a versatile VPN solution that supports various VPN protocols, including IPsec and IKEv2, for establishing secure tunnels between devices. By configuring the strongswan service with a custom configuration file and deploying appropriate IPsec policies, administrators can deploy scalable VPN solutions with advanced features such as multi-site connectivity, certificate-based authentication, and dynamic routing, ensuring secure and reliable communication across distributed networks. Additionally, the wireguard command is a modern VPN protocol that offers high-performance, secure tunneling capabilities with minimal overhead. By installing the WireGuard kernel module and configuring the wireguard service with peer-to-peer connections and encryption keys, administrators can deploy lightweight and efficient VPN solutions for secure communication between devices, enhancing network privacy and performance. Furthermore, the openconnect command is a client for connecting to Cisco AnyConnect VPN servers, which are widely used *in enterprise environments for remote access and secure connectivity. By running the openconnect command with options such as -u for specifying the username or -b for running in the background, administrators can establish encrypted VPN connections to Cisco AnyConnect servers, enabling authorized users to access corporate resources securely from remote locations.*

Chapter 7: Scaling Network Resources for Performance and Efficiency

Horizontal and vertical scaling strategies are essential considerations for ensuring the scalability and performance of applications and services in modern computing environments. Horizontal scaling, also known as scaling out, involves adding more instances of resources such as servers or containers to distribute the workload across multiple machines. One common CLI command for horizontal scaling is docker-compose, which is used to manage multi-container Docker applications. By running the docker-compose command followed by the up option and specifying the desired number of replicas or instances for each service in the docker-compose.yml file, administrators can horizontally scale Dockerized applications to handle increased traffic or workload demands. Additionally, cloud providers offer auto-scaling services such as AWS Auto Scaling or Azure Autoscale, which automatically adjust the number of virtual machines or instances based on predefined metrics such as CPU utilization or network traffic. By configuring auto-scaling policies and thresholds using the respective cloud provider's CLI tools or management consoles, administrators can enable horizontal scaling for cloud-based applications and services, ensuring optimal performance and resource utilization. Moreover, container orchestration platforms like Kubernetes provide built-in support for horizontal scaling through features such as the Horizontal Pod Autoscaler (HPA). By defining HPA objects in Kubernetes manifests and specifying resource metrics such as CPU or memory utilization, administrators can automatically scale the number of pod replicas to match the current workload requirements. By using the kubectl command-line tool to apply HPA manifests and monitor scaling events, administrators can efficiently manage the horizontal scaling of containerized workloads in Kubernetes clusters, ensuring high availability and performance for microservices-based applications. Furthermore, load balancers play a crucial role in horizontal scaling by distributing incoming traffic evenly across multiple instances or nodes. Cloud providers offer managed load balancing services such as AWS Elastic Load Balancing (ELB) or Google Cloud Load Balancing, which automatically scale and distribute traffic to backend instances based on predefined routing rules and health checks. By using CLI commands such as aws elb or gcloud compute, administrators can configure and manage load balancers to support horizontal scaling for web applications, APIs, and microservices deployed in cloud environments, ensuring fault tolerance and optimal performance under varying traffic conditions. Additionally, traditional web servers like Nginx or Apache HTTP Server support load balancing capabilities through *modules such as Nginx Plus or Apache HTTP Server with mod_proxy_balancer. By configuring load balancing directives in the server configuration files and specifying backend server pools, administrators can implement horizontal scaling for web applications or services hosted on traditional server infrastructure, ensuring efficient resource utilization and high availability. Moreover, content delivery networks (CDNs) play a vital role in horizontal scaling by caching and serving static content from edge locations distributed worldwide. Cloud-based CDNs such as Amazon CloudFront or Google Cloud CDN leverage global networks of edge servers to deliver content to end-users with low latency and high throughput. By using CLI commands such as aws cloudfront or gcloud compute cdn, administrators can configure and manage CDN distributions to scale horizontally and offload traffic from origin servers, ensuring fast and reliable content delivery for web applications and media streaming services. Furthermore, serverless computing platforms like AWS Lambda or Google Cloud Functions offer a serverless approach to horizontal scaling by automatically provisioning and managing compute resources based on event-driven triggers. By deploying functions or microservices as serverless applications and defining triggers such as HTTP requests or message queue events, administrators can enable automatic scaling of compute resources to handle incoming workload spikes or concurrent requests. By using CLI commands such as aws lambda or gcloud functions, administrators can deploy serverless functions and configure scaling parameters to optimize resource utilization and minimize costs, ensuring efficient and elastic scalability for event-driven workloads. Additionally, database systems play a critical role in horizontal scaling by supporting distributed architectures and sharding techniques to partition data across multiple nodes. NoSQL databases like MongoDB or Cassandra offer built-in support for horizontal scaling through features such as sharding or replication. By using CLI commands or management consoles provided by database vendors, administrators can configure and manage database clusters to horizontally scale storage and processing capacity, ensuring high availability and performance for data-intensive applications and analytics workloads. Moreover, distributed caching systems like Redis or Memcached serve as a key component of horizontal scaling strategies by offloading database and application server loads. By deploying caching clusters and configuring cache eviction policies and replication settings, administrators can improve application performance and scalability by caching frequently accessed data in memory. By using CLI commands such as redis-cli or memcached-tool, administrators can monitor cache usage, manage cache clusters, and troubleshoot caching issues to optimize application performance and reduce database load, ensuring efficient horizontal scaling for* data-driven applications and services. Additionally, message queueing systems such as RabbitMQ or Apache Kafka enable asynchronous communication and workload distribution across distributed components in modern application architectures. By deploying message brokers and defining message queues or topics, administrators can decouple components, distribute tasks, and scale horizontally to handle varying workloads or processing requirements. Auto-scaling configurations with CLI automation are pivotal components of modern cloud infrastructure management, enabling dynamic resource allocation based on workload demands to ensure optimal performance and cost efficiency. One essential tool for implementing auto-scaling configurations is AWS CLI, which provides a comprehensive set of commands for automating the deployment and management of auto-scaling groups in Amazon EC2. By utilizing the autoscaling command, administrators can create auto-scaling groups, define scaling policies, and set up triggers based on metrics such as CPU utilization or network traffic. For instance, to create an auto-scaling group named "my-asg" with a desired capacity of 5 instances, administrators can use the following command: aws autoscaling create-auto-scaling-group --auto-scaling-group-name my-asg --launch-configuration-name my-launch-config --min-size 1 --max-size 10 --desired-capacity 5. Additionally, administrators can configure scaling policies using the put-scaling-policy command, specifying parameters such as the scaling adjustment and cooldown period. For example, to create a scaling policy that adds 2 instances when CPU utilization exceeds 70%, administrators can use the following command: aws autoscaling put-scaling-policy --auto-scaling-group-name my-asg --policy-name my-scaling-policy --scaling-adjustment 2 --adjustment-type ChangeInCapacity --cooldown 300 --metric-name CPUUtilization --threshold 70 --comparison-operator GreaterThanThreshold. Moreover, CLI automation tools like Terraform provide infrastructure as code capabilities for managing auto-scaling configurations across multi-cloud environments. By defining auto-scaling resources in Terraform configuration files, administrators can leverage the terraform apply command to provision and update auto-scaling groups, scaling policies, and associated resources in a declarative and consistent manner. For example, a Terraform configuration snippet for creating an auto-scaling group could look like this:

hclCopy code

```
resource "aws_auto_scaling_group" "my_asg" { name = "my-asg" launch_configuration = aws_launch_configuration.my_launch_config.name
min_size = 1 max_size = 10 desired_capacity = 5 }
resource "aws_autoscaling_policy" "my_scaling_policy" { name = "my-scaling-policy" scaling_adjustment = 2 adjustment_type = "ChangeInCapacity" cooldown = 300 autoscaling_group_name =
```

aws_auto_scaling_group.my_asg.name
metric_aggregation_type   =   "Average"
estimated_instance_warmup   =   300
target_tracking_configuration   {
predefined_metric_specification   {
predefined_metric_type   =
"ASGAverageCPUUtilization" target_value = 70 } } }
By running terraform apply, Terraform will automatically create or update the specified auto-scaling resources based on the configuration defined in the .tf files. Additionally, cloud-native container orchestration platforms like Kubernetes offer built-in support for horizontal pod auto-scaling (HPA), allowing administrators to automatically scale containerized workloads based on resource utilization metrics. Using the kubectl command-line tool, administrators can create HPA objects and specify scaling policies to dynamically adjust the number of pod replicas. For example, to create an HPA that scales based on CPU utilization, administrators can use the following command: kubectl autoscale deployment my-deployment --cpu-percent=70 --min=1 --max=10. This command sets up an HPA for the my-deployment deployment, scaling the number of replicas between 1 and 10 based on CPU utilization exceeding 70%. Furthermore, cloud providers offer managed auto-scaling services that simplify the configuration and management of auto-scaling configurations. For instance, AWS Auto Scaling provides a unified interface for defining scaling

policies across various AWS services such as EC2, DynamoDB, and ECS. Administrators can use the AWS Management Console or AWS CLI to create scaling plans, define scaling policies, and automate the scaling of resources based on predefined triggers and metrics. Similarly, Google Cloud offers Cloud Monitoring and Cloud Scheduler services that allow administrators to define autoscaling policies and schedule scaling actions based on custom or predefined metrics. By using the gcloud command-line tool, administrators can configure auto-scaling policies and triggers for Google Cloud Platform (GCP) resources such as Compute Engine instances, Kubernetes Engine clusters, and App Engine services. For example, to create an autoscaling policy for a Compute Engine instance group, administrators can use the following command: gcloud compute instance-groups managed set-autoscaling my-instance-group --max-num-replicas=10 --min-num-replicas=1 --target-cpu-utilization=0.6. This command sets up an autoscaling policy for the my-instance-group instance group, scaling the number of replicas between 1 and 10 based on CPU utilization reaching 60%. Moreover, administrators can leverage scripting languages like Python or Bash to automate the deployment and management of auto-scaling configurations.

Chapter 8: Advanced Network Monitoring and Alerting Systems

Customizing network monitoring dashboards is crucial for organizations to gain actionable insights into the health, performance, and security of their network infrastructure. One powerful tool for creating customizable dashboards is Grafana, which allows administrators to visualize data from various sources and tailor dashboards to meet specific monitoring requirements. By utilizing the Grafana web interface or CLI commands, administrators can create new dashboards, add panels, and configure data sources to display real-time metrics and trends. For example, to create a new dashboard named "Network Monitoring," administrators can use the following CLI command: grafana-cli admin reset-admin-password <new-password>. This command resets the admin password for accessing the Grafana web interface. After logging in, administrators can navigate to the dashboard section and create a new dashboard with the desired layout and visualization panels. Additionally, Grafana supports integration with popular monitoring systems such as Prometheus, InfluxDB, and Elasticsearch, allowing administrators to aggregate and visualize data from multiple sources in a single dashboard. By configuring data source settings in Grafana and specifying query parameters, administrators can pull metrics and logs from backend systems and display them in customizable panels. For example, to add a Prometheus data source named "PrometheusServer" to Grafana, administrators can use the following CLI command: grafana-cli admin reset-admin-password <new-password>. This command resets the admin password for accessing the Grafana web interface. After logging in, administrators can navigate to the data sources section and add a new Prometheus data source with the URL of the Prometheus server and authentication settings if required. Once the data source is configured, administrators can create dashboard panels and query data from Prometheus using PromQL (Prometheus Query Language) to visualize network metrics such as throughput, latency, and error rates. Moreover, Grafana provides a wide range of visualization options and customization features, allowing administrators to create interactive and informative dashboards tailored to their specific monitoring needs. By selecting from various panel types such as graphs, gauges, tables, and heatmaps, administrators can present network data in a visually appealing and meaningful way. Additionally, Grafana supports templating and variable substitution, enabling *administrators to create dynamic dashboards that adapt to changing environments or user preferences. For example, administrators can use template variables to filter data by time range, hostname, or service name, providing users with the flexibility to customize dashboard views based on their requirements. Furthermore, Grafana offers alerting capabilities that allow administrators to define threshold-based alerts and notifications for important network events or anomalies. By configuring alert rules in Grafana and specifying alert conditions, administrators can trigger notifications via email, Slack, or other channels when predefined thresholds are exceeded. For example, administrators can create an alert rule to monitor network latency and send an email notification if the latency exceeds a certain threshold for a specified duration. Additionally, Grafana supports integration with external alerting services such as PagerDuty, OpsGenie, and VictorOps, enabling administrators to escalate and manage alerts through third-party incident management platforms. This integration allows organizations to streamline their alerting and incident response workflows and ensure timely resolution of network issues. Moreover, Grafana provides extensive support for user authentication and access control, allowing administrators to define roles and permissions for dashboard users. By integrating Grafana with LDAP, OAuth, or SAML authentication providers, administrators can authenticate users against existing identity management systems and enforce fine-grained access control policies based on user roles or groups. Additionally, Grafana supports integration with external authorization providers such as Okta, Azure AD, and Keycloak, enabling administrators to enforce access policies based on user attributes or group memberships. This integration allows organizations to centralize user authentication and authorization processes and ensure secure access to network monitoring dashboards and data. Furthermore, Grafana offers built-in support for dashboard versioning and revision history, allowing administrators to track changes made to dashboards over time and revert to previous versions if needed. By enabling version control in Grafana settings, administrators can create new dashboard revisions with each change and compare different versions to identify modifications or discrepancies. Additionally, Grafana supports exporting and importing dashboards in JSON format, allowing administrators to share dashboards between instances or backup dashboard configurations for disaster recovery purposes. This feature enables organizations to maintain consistency across multiple Grafana deployments and ensure continuity of network monitoring operations. Moreover, Grafana provides integration with collaboration platforms such as GitHub and GitLab, allowing administrators to manage dashboard configurations as code and leverage version control workflows for collaborative dashboard development and deployment. By storing dashboard configurations in version-controlled repositories, administrators can track changes, review pull requests, and automate deployment pipelines using continuous integration and continuous deployment (CI/CD) practices. This integration simplifies the management of complex dashboard configurations and ensures consistency across development, staging, and production environments. Additionally, Grafana offers extensive documentation and community support, enabling administrators to leverage tutorials, guides, and forums for troubleshooting issues, sharing best practices, and learning advanced features. By accessing the Grafana documentation website or joining community forums such as the Grafana community forum or Reddit, administrators can tap into a wealth of resources and expertise to maximize the effectiveness of their network monitoring dashboards. Setting up proactive alerting systems with CLI is essential for organizations to detect and respond to potential issues in their Azure networking environment before they escalate into critical problems. One effective approach to achieve proactive alerting is by leveraging Azure Monitor and its associated services such as Azure Log Analytics and Azure Monitor Alerts. By utilizing the Azure CLI, administrators can configure monitoring rules and thresholds to trigger alerts based on predefined conditions and thresholds. For instance, to enable Azure Monitor for a virtual network, administrators can use the command az monitor enable, which activates monitoring capabilities and starts collecting telemetry data from network resources. After enabling Azure Monitor, administrators can define custom log queries using Kusto Query Language (KQL) to filter and analyze network-related data such as traffic patterns, packet drops, and resource utilization. By crafting queries to identify specific events or anomalies indicative of network issues, administrators can create proactive alerting rules to notify stakeholders when predefined conditions are met. For example, to create an alert rule that triggers an alert when network traffic exceeds a certain threshold, administrators can use the command az monitor alert create, specifying parameters such as the target resource, condition, and alert action. Additionally, administrators can leverage metric-based alerts to monitor performance metrics such as latency, throughput, and error rates and trigger alerts when deviations from baseline values occur.*

By using the command az monitor metrics alert create, administrators can define alert criteria based on metric values and configure notification channels to alert relevant stakeholders via email, SMS, or webhook. Furthermore, administrators can implement proactive alerting for security-related events by integrating Azure Security Center with Azure Monitor. By enabling Security Center recommendations and configuring security policies, administrators can detect and remediate security vulnerabilities and compliance issues in real-time. For example, to enable Security Center recommendations for network security groups (NSGs), administrators can use the command az security pricing create to enable Security Center standard pricing tier, which includes advanced security features such as threat detection, vulnerability assessment, and just-in-time access. After enabling Security Center, administrators can configure security policies to monitor NSG configurations and alert on policy violations such as open ports, unauthorized access, or insecure network configurations. Additionally, administrators can integrate Azure Sentinel, Microsoft's cloud-native SIEM (Security Information and Event Management) solution, with Azure Monitor to enhance proactive threat detection and response capabilities. By ingesting security logs and telemetry data from Azure Monitor into Azure Sentinel, administrators can correlate security events across their Azure environment and detect advanced threats and suspicious activities. For example, to onboard Azure Monitor logs to Azure Sentinel, administrators can use the command az monitor log-analytics workspace get-shared-keys to retrieve the workspace ID and primary key of the target Log Analytics workspace, and then use the command az monitor diagnostic-settings create to configure log forwarding to Azure Sentinel. Once Azure Monitor logs are ingested into Azure Sentinel, administrators can create custom alert rules and playbooks to automate incident response workflows and mitigate security incidents proactively. Moreover, administrators can leverage Azure Automation and Azure Functions to implement custom alerting and remediation workflows in response to specific network events or conditions. By creating runbooks and automation scripts using PowerShell or Python, administrators can define proactive response actions to address common network issues such as network connectivity failures, DNS resolution errors, or resource depletion. For instance, to create an Azure Automation runbook that automatically restarts a virtual machine when network connectivity is lost, administrators can use the command az vm run-command invoke to execute a PowerShell script on the target VM, which checks network connectivity and restarts the VM if *necessary. Additionally, administrators can deploy Azure Functions with event-driven triggers to respond to network alerts in real-time and execute predefined actions such as scaling resources, updating network configurations, or sending notifications to stakeholders. By leveraging serverless compute capabilities, administrators can implement lightweight and scalable alerting and remediation workflows that minimize operational overhead and ensure rapid response to network events. In summary, setting up proactive alerting systems with CLI empowers organizations to detect, analyze, and respond to network issues effectively, mitigating potential impacts on performance, security, and reliability. By leveraging Azure Monitor, Azure Security Center, Azure Sentinel, and automation tools such as Azure Automation and Azure Functions, administrators can implement custom alerting rules, automate response actions, and enhance the overall resilience of their Azure networking environment.*

Chapter 9: Optimizing Data Transfer and Bandwidth Usage

Implementing traffic optimization techniques is crucial for organizations to ensure efficient utilization of network resources and enhance the overall performance and reliability of their applications and services. One effective approach to traffic optimization is by leveraging Azure Front Door, a scalable and secure global content delivery network (CDN) service that enables organizations to accelerate web applications, APIs, and content delivery to users worldwide. By using the Azure CLI, administrators can deploy and configure Azure Front Door to optimize traffic routing, improve latency, and enhance the user experience. For example, to create an Azure Front Door instance, administrators can use the command az network front-door create, specifying parameters such as the resource group, name, and frontend host name. After creating the Front Door instance, administrators can configure routing rules, caching policies, and load-balancing settings to optimize traffic distribution and reduce latency. Additionally, administrators can leverage Azure Traffic Manager, a DNS-based traffic management service, to optimize traffic routing across multiple Azure regions and endpoints. By using the command az network traffic-manager profile create, administrators can create a

Traffic Manager profile and define routing methods such as priority, weighted, or performance-based routing to distribute traffic based on proximity, latency, or endpoint health. Moreover, administrators can implement traffic optimization techniques at the application layer by using Azure Application Gateway, a layer 7 load balancer that provides advanced traffic management capabilities for web applications. By using the command az network application-gateway create, administrators can deploy an Application Gateway instance and configure features such as URL-based routing, SSL termination, and web application firewall (WAF) to optimize traffic flow and protect against common web threats. Furthermore, administrators can optimize traffic for containerized workloads by deploying Azure Kubernetes Service (AKS) clusters and leveraging Kubernetes-native features such as horizontal pod autoscaling, pod affinity, and service mesh integration. By using the command az aks create, administrators can create an AKS cluster and configure features such as auto-scaling, network policies, and ingress controllers to optimize traffic routing and ensure high availability and scalability for containerized applications. Additionally, administrators can use Azure CDN, a globally distributed network of edge servers, to cache and deliver content closer to end-users, reducing latency and improving performance for web applications and media streaming services. By using the command az cdn profile create, administrators can create a CDN profile and configure endpoints, caching rules, and geo-filtering settings to optimize content delivery and accelerate web page load times. Moreover, administrators can implement traffic optimization techniques for virtual network (VNet) connectivity by using Azure Virtual WAN, a networking service that provides optimized and automated branch-to-branch connectivity for distributed organizations. By using the command az network vpn-gateway create, administrators can deploy a Virtual WAN hub and configure VPN gateways, route tables, and traffic filters to optimize network traffic routing and ensure secure and reliable connectivity between branch offices and cloud resources. Additionally, administrators can optimize traffic for hybrid cloud environments by using Azure ExpressRoute, a dedicated private connection to Azure data centers. By using the command az network express-route create, administrators can provision an ExpressRoute circuit and configure peering, routing, and bandwidth settings to optimize traffic flow and ensure low-latency, high-throughput connectivity between on-premises data centers and Azure services. In summary, implementing traffic optimization techniques with CLI empowers organizations to improve the performance, reliability, and scalability of their network infrastructure and applications. By leveraging services such as Azure Front Door, Traffic Manager, Application Gateway, AKS, CDN, Virtual WAN, and ExpressRoute, administrators can optimize *traffic routing, reduce latency, and enhance the overall user experience for customers and end-users worldwide. Bandwidth management and throttling strategies are essential components of network optimization and resource allocation, enabling organizations to efficiently manage and prioritize network traffic to meet performance requirements and prevent network congestion. One effective approach to bandwidth management is by implementing Quality of Service (QoS) policies, which allow administrators to prioritize certain types of traffic over others based on predefined rules and criteria. By using the Azure CLI, administrators can deploy QoS policies to allocate bandwidth resources and enforce traffic prioritization across their network infrastructure. For example, administrators can use the command az network vnet create to create a virtual network (VNet) and specify parameters such as the resource group, name, and address prefixes. Once the VNet is created, administrators can configure QoS policies for specific subnets within the VNet by using the command az network vnet subnet update and specifying parameters such as the subnet name and the desired QoS settings, including minimum and maximum bandwidth limits, priority levels, and traffic shaping algorithms. Additionally, administrators can implement bandwidth management and throttling strategies at the application layer by using Azure Application Gateway, a layer 7 load balancer that provides advanced traffic management capabilities* for web applications. By using the command az network application-gateway create, administrators can deploy an Application Gateway instance and configure features such as request-based routing, SSL termination, and connection draining to manage incoming traffic and prevent overloading backend servers. Moreover, administrators can leverage Azure Content Delivery Network (CDN) to distribute content and media files efficiently to end-users worldwide while reducing bandwidth consumption and optimizing network performance. By using the command az cdn endpoint create, administrators can create a CDN endpoint and configure caching policies, compression settings, and geo-filtering rules to minimize data transfer costs and improve content delivery speed. Furthermore, administrators can implement bandwidth management and throttling strategies for hybrid cloud environments by using Azure ExpressRoute, a dedicated private connection to Azure data centers. By using the command az network express-route create, administrators can provision an ExpressRoute circuit and configure bandwidth settings, including burst limits and maximum data transfer rates, to control network traffic flow and ensure consistent performance for mission-critical workloads. Additionally, administrators can leverage Azure Traffic Manager, a DNS-based traffic management service, to distribute incoming requests across multiple Azure regions and endpoints based on performance, availability, and geographic proximity.

By using the command *az network traffic-manager profile create*, administrators can create a Traffic Manager profile and configure routing methods such as priority, weighted, or performance-based routing to optimize traffic distribution and minimize latency. In summary, bandwidth management and throttling strategies are essential for optimizing network performance, ensuring resource availability, and enhancing the overall user experience. By leveraging QoS policies, Application Gateway, CDN, ExpressRoute, and Traffic Manager, administrators can effectively manage network traffic, prioritize critical workloads, and mitigate potential bottlenecks to achieve reliable and efficient network operations.

Chapter 10: Advanced Network Access Control and Authentication Methods

Multi-Factor Authentication (MFA) is a crucial security measure that adds an extra layer of protection to user accounts by requiring multiple forms of verification before granting access. With the Azure CLI, administrators can configure MFA settings to enhance the security posture of their Azure environment. The first step in setting up MFA is to enable it for Azure Active Directory (AD) users. This can be achieved using the command az ad user update --id <user-object-id> --password-policies DisablePasswordExpiration DisableStrongPassword. Once MFA is enabled for users, administrators can configure the authentication methods required for verification, such as phone call, text message, or mobile app notification. This can be done using the command az ad user update --id <user-object-id> --add AuthenticationMethod. Additionally, administrators can enforce MFA for specific Azure AD roles or groups to ensure that privileged accounts have an added layer of protection. This can be accomplished using the command az ad group update --id <group-object-id> --add AdditionalData.authenticationMethods. Furthermore, administrators can define conditional access policies to enforce MFA based on specific criteria such as user location, device type, or risk level. This can be achieved using the command *az ad user update --id <user-object-id> --add AdditionalData.conditions*. By implementing MFA, organizations can significantly reduce the risk of unauthorized access and mitigate the impact of potential security breaches. However, it is essential to strike a balance between security and usability to ensure that MFA does not impede user productivity. Administrators should carefully consider factors such as user experience, authentication methods, and enforcement policies when configuring MFA settings. Additionally, organizations should educate users about the importance of MFA and provide clear instructions on how to set up and use MFA to protect their accounts. By promoting awareness and adoption of MFA best practices, organizations can strengthen their overall security posture and safeguard sensitive data and resources from unauthorized access. In summary, MFA is a critical security measure that provides an additional layer of protection against unauthorized access to Azure resources. With the Azure CLI, administrators can easily configure and manage MFA settings to enhance security and protect against evolving cybersecurity threats. By implementing MFA and promoting security awareness among users, organizations can reduce the risk of security breaches and safeguard their valuable assets in the cloud.

Implementing network access policies and segmentation is essential for maintaining the security *and integrity of an organization's network infrastructure. With Azure Networking, administrators can enforce granular access controls and segment their network to mitigate the risk of unauthorized access and lateral movement within the network. The first step in implementing network access policies and segmentation is to define security groups and access control lists (ACLs) to regulate traffic flow between different network segments. This can be achieved using the Azure CLI by creating network security groups (NSGs) and associating them with subnets or network interfaces. For example, the command az network nsg create can be used to create a new NSG, and az network nsg rule create can be used to define specific rules for inbound and outbound traffic. By configuring NSG rules, administrators can restrict communication between different segments of the network based on criteria such as source IP address, destination IP address, port number, and protocol. Additionally, administrators can implement virtual network peering to establish secure communication between virtual networks and enable cross-network access without exposing sensitive resources to the public internet. This can be accomplished using the command az network vnet peering create to create a peering connection between two virtual networks and az network vnet peering update to configure the peering settings, such as traffic forwarding and access permissions. By leveraging virtual network peering, organizations can create a secure and isolated network environment while facilitating seamless communication between interconnected resources. Furthermore, administrators can implement network segmentation by deploying multiple subnets within a virtual network and applying NSG rules to control traffic between subnets. This allows organizations to compartmentalize their network infrastructure and enforce access policies based on the principle of least privilege. For example, sensitive workloads or resources can be placed in separate subnets with stricter access controls to minimize the risk of unauthorized access. Moreover, administrators can utilize Azure Firewall to centrally manage and enforce network security policies across their virtual networks. Azure Firewall provides stateful network and application layer protection, threat intelligence integration, and customizable rules to secure inbound and outbound traffic. By deploying Azure Firewall, organizations can achieve centralized visibility and control over network traffic, ensuring consistent enforcement of security policies across their Azure environment. Additionally, administrators can leverage Azure Bastion to securely access virtual machines (VMs) within their virtual networks without exposing RDP or SSH ports to the public internet. Azure Bastion provides a fully managed, PaaS-based solution for secure and seamless RDP/SSH connectivity to VMs, eliminating the need for bastion hosts or VPN gateways. By deploying Azure Bastion, organizations can strengthen their network security posture and* mitigate the risk of credential theft and unauthorized access to VMs. In summary, implementing network access policies and segmentation is critical for securing Azure Networking environments and protecting against cyber threats. By leveraging Azure CLI commands and native Azure Networking features such as NSGs, virtual network peering, Azure Firewall, and Azure Bastion, administrators can enforce granular access controls, segment their network infrastructure, and mitigate the risk of unauthorized access and lateral movement within the network. By adopting a proactive approach to network security and following best practices for access control and segmentation, organizations can effectively safeguard their Azure resources and data from cyber threats.

BOOK 4
AZURE NETWORKING ARCHITECT
EXPERT STRATEGIES AND BEST PRACTICES FOR CLI
POWER USERS

ROB BOTWRIGHT

Chapter 1: Architectural Principles for Azure Networking

Understanding Azure Network Design Fundamentals is crucial for architects and administrators tasked with designing and implementing network infrastructure in Azure. At the core of Azure network design is the Azure Virtual Network (VNet), which serves as the foundation for connecting and isolating Azure resources. To create a VNet using the Azure CLI, administrators can use the command az network vnet create. When designing a VNet, considerations such as address space, subnetting, and region placement are essential. Address space defines the range of IP addresses that can be assigned to resources within the VNet and should be carefully planned to avoid IP address conflicts. Subnetting allows administrators to divide the VNet into smaller, more manageable subnets, each serving a specific purpose or workload. This can be achieved using the command az network vnet subnet create to create individual subnets within the VNet. When deploying resources within a VNet, administrators must consider the placement of these resources in different regions to optimize performance and availability. Azure Availability Zones provide high availability and fault tolerance by distributing resources across multiple datacenters within a region. To deploy resources across Availability Zones, administrators can specify the desired zone using the --zone parameter when creating resources such as VMs or load balancers. Additionally, administrators can leverage Azure Virtual Network Peering to establish private and secure connectivity between VNets in the same region or across different regions. Peering connections can be created using the command az network vnet peering create, allowing resources in peered VNets to communicate with each other as if they were on the same network. When designing network security in Azure, administrators must implement robust security controls to protect against cyber threats and unauthorized access. Network Security Groups (NSGs) are essential for enforcing network security policies by filtering inbound and outbound traffic to and from Azure resources. NSGs can be created using the command az network nsg create and associated with subnets or network interfaces to control traffic flow based on source and destination IP addresses, port numbers, and protocols. Additionally, Azure Firewall provides an enterprise-grade firewall solution for securing inbound and outbound traffic to virtual networks. Azure Firewall can be deployed using the command az network firewall create and configured with application rules, network rules, and threat intelligence feeds to protect against known and emerging threats. When designing for performance and scalability, administrators must consider factors such as network bandwidth, latency, and throughput. Azure ExpressRoute provides a dedicated, private connection to Azure datacenters, offering higher reliability, lower latency, and greater security compared to public internet connections. To deploy Azure ExpressRoute, administrators can use the command az network express-route create and specify the desired bandwidth and peering locations. Additionally, administrators can optimize network performance using Azure Traffic Manager, which enables global load balancing and routing based on endpoint health and geographic proximity. Traffic Manager profiles can be created using the command az network traffic-manager profile create and configured with routing methods such as priority, weighted, or geographic routing. In summary, understanding Azure Network Design Fundamentals is essential for architecting secure, scalable, and high-performance network infrastructure in Azure. By leveraging the Azure CLI and native Azure networking services such as Virtual Network, Network Security Groups, Azure Firewall, ExpressRoute, and Traffic Manager, administrators can design and deploy robust network architectures that meet the requirements of their organizations and ensure the reliability and security of their Azure *resources.*

Designing for scalability, flexibility, and performance in cloud environments is crucial for meeting the evolving needs of modern applications and workloads. One key aspect of designing for scalability is to leverage cloud-native services and architectures that can dynamically scale resources based on demand. In Azure, services like Azure Kubernetes Service (AKS) provide a managed Kubernetes environment that automatically scales the underlying infrastructure to accommodate changes in workload traffic. Administrators can deploy AKS clusters using the command az aks create and configure autoscaling settings to automatically adjust the number of pods based on CPU or memory utilization. Additionally, Azure App Service offers a fully managed platform for building, deploying, and scaling web applications without managing the underlying infrastructure. Administrators can create an App Service plan using the command az appservice plan create and deploy applications to the plan, allowing Azure to automatically scale the underlying resources based on workload demands. Another key consideration for scalability is to design for elasticity, which involves the ability to dynamically provision and de-provision resources in response to changing workload requirements. Azure Virtual Machine Scale Sets enable administrators to create and manage a group of identical, auto-scaling VMs that automatically scale in or out based on metrics such as CPU usage or incoming requests. Scale sets can be created using the command az vmss create and configured with scaling policies to ensure optimal resource utilization. Additionally, Azure Database Services such as Azure SQL Database and Azure Cosmos DB offer built-in scaling capabilities that allow databases to automatically adjust performance levels based on workload demand. Administrators can configure autoscaling for Azure SQL Database using the command az sql db update and specifying the desired service tier and performance level. When designing for flexibility, it's essential to adopt a modular and decoupled architecture that allows for easy integration and evolution of components. Azure Functions provide a serverless compute service that allows administrators to run code in response to events without provisioning or managing servers. Functions can be deployed using the command az functionapp create and configured to trigger based on various events such as HTTP requests, timers, or message queue triggers. Additionally, Azure Logic Apps offer a workflow automation service that enables administrators to orchestrate and automate tasks across different Azure services and external systems. Logic Apps can be created using the command az logic workflow create and configured with triggers and actions to automate business processes. Another aspect of designing for flexibility is to embrace microservices architectures, which involve breaking down applications into smaller, loosely coupled services that can be independently developed, deployed, and scaled. Azure Service Fabric is a distributed systems platform that enables administrators to build and deploy microservices-based applications with ease. Service Fabric clusters can be created using the command az sf cluster create and configured to host stateful or stateless services that can scale independently based on workload demands. Finally, when designing for performance, it's essential to optimize resource utilization and minimize latency by leveraging caching, content delivery networks (CDNs), and performance monitoring tools. Azure Cache for Redis is a fully managed in-memory data store that enables administrators to build highly scalable and responsive applications by caching frequently accessed data. Redis caches can be created using the command az redis create and configured with features such as data persistence, clustering, and geo-replication to enhance performance and availability. Additionally, Azure CDN is a global content delivery network that accelerates the delivery of web content to users worldwide by caching content at edge locations closer to end-users. Administrators can enable CDN for Azure *resources using the command az cdn endpoint create and configure caching rules and optimizations to improve performance and reduce latency. Lastly, administrators can use Azure Monitor to gain insights into the performance and health of their Azure resources by collecting and analyzing metrics, logs, and traces. Azure Monitor resources can be created using the command az monitor create and configured to monitor various aspects of Azure services such as VMs, databases, and applications. By designing for scalability, flexibility, and performance and leveraging cloud-native services and architectures in Azure, administrators can build resilient and high-performing applications that meet the demands of their organizations and customers.*

Chapter 2: Designing Scalable and Resilient Network Architectures

Implementing redundancy and fault tolerance is crucial for ensuring high availability and reliability in cloud-based systems. Redundancy involves the duplication of critical components or systems to minimize the risk of a single point of failure, while fault tolerance focuses on the system's ability to continue operating properly in the event of component failures or other unforeseen issues. In Azure, several services and strategies can be leveraged to implement redundancy and fault tolerance effectively. One common approach is to deploy resources across multiple Azure regions to mitigate the impact of regional failures. Azure provides a global network of data centers distributed across multiple geographic regions, allowing administrators to deploy resources in different regions using the Azure CLI. For example, to create a virtual machine in a specific Azure region, the command az vm create can be used with the --location parameter to specify the desired region. By deploying resources across multiple regions, administrators can ensure that their applications remain accessible and operational even if an entire region becomes unavailable due to a disaster or outage. Additionally, Azure offers built-in redundancy and fault tolerance features for many of its services, such as Azure Storage and Azure SQL Database. Azure Storage provides multiple redundancy options, including locally redundant storage (LRS), geo-redundant storage (GRS), and zone-redundant storage (ZRS), each offering varying levels of redundancy and fault tolerance. Administrators can configure redundancy options when creating storage accounts using the az storage account create command and specifying the desired redundancy type. Similarly, Azure SQL Database offers built-in high availability and fault tolerance with features like automatic backups, automated failover, and geo-replication. Administrators can enable these features when creating or configuring SQL databases using the Azure CLI commands az sql db create and az sql db update. Another important aspect of implementing redundancy and fault tolerance is designing applications with resiliency in mind. This involves architecting applications to gracefully handle failures and recover quickly without impacting the user experience. Azure provides several services and patterns that can help developers build resilient applications, such as Azure App Service's built-in load balancing and auto-scaling capabilities. Administrators can deploy highly available web applications using Azure App Service by creating an

App Service plan with multiple instances using the az appservice plan create command and deploying the application code to the plan using the az webapp create command. Additionally, Azure Traffic Manager is a DNS-based traffic load balancer that enables administrators to distribute incoming traffic across multiple Azure regions or endpoints based on various routing methods, including performance, priority, and geographic proximity. Administrators can configure Traffic Manager profiles and endpoints using the Azure CLI commands az network traffic-manager profile create and az network traffic-manager endpoint create, allowing them to implement redundancy and fault tolerance for their applications. Moreover, Azure Virtual Machine Scale Sets (VMSS) enable administrators to deploy and manage a group of identical, auto-scaling virtual machines that automatically scale in or out based on demand or health metrics. VMSS can be created using the az vmss create command and configured with scaling policies and health probes to ensure high availability and fault tolerance. Additionally, Azure Load Balancer is a layer 4 (TCP, UDP) load balancer that distributes incoming network traffic across multiple VMs in a backend pool to ensure high availability and fault tolerance. Administrators can create load balancer resources using the az network lb create command and configure backend pools and health probes to distribute traffic effectively. In summary, implementing redundancy and fault tolerance in Azure involves leveraging the platform's global infrastructure, built-in redundancy features, and resilient application design patterns to ensure high availability and reliability for cloud-based systems. By deploying resources across multiple regions, leveraging built-in redundancy features, and designing applications for resiliency, administrators can minimize the impact of failures and disruptions and maintain uninterrupted service availability for their users. Building highly available network infrastructures is essential for ensuring uninterrupted connectivity and reliable access to resources in modern IT environments. In Azure, administrators can leverage various services and configurations to design and deploy highly available network infrastructures that can withstand failures and maintain service continuity. One fundamental aspect of building a highly available network infrastructure is designing redundant architectures that eliminate single points of failure and provide failover capabilities. This can be achieved by deploying redundant instances of critical components such as virtual machines, network appliances, and load balancers across multiple availability zones or regions. Azure Virtual Machines (VMs) offer several options for redundancy and fault tolerance, including Availability Sets and Virtual Machine Scale Sets

(VMSS). Availability Sets ensure that VM instances are distributed across multiple fault domains and update domains within a datacenter, minimizing the impact of hardware failures and planned maintenance events. Administrators can create an Availability Set using the az vm availability-set create command and then deploy VMs to the set using the az vm create command with the --availability-set parameter. Additionally, VMSS allows administrators to deploy and manage a group of identical, auto-scaling VMs across multiple availability zones or regions, ensuring high availability and scalability. VMSS can be created using the az vmss create command and configured with scaling policies and health probes to automatically scale in or out based on demand or health metrics. Azure Load Balancer is another critical component for building highly available network infrastructures. It distributes incoming network traffic across multiple VMs or instances in a backend pool to ensure high availability and fault tolerance. Administrators can create a basic load balancer using the az network lb create command or a standard load balancer with additional features such as high availability sets and zone-redundant frontends using the az network lb create command with specific parameters. Azure Traffic Manager is a DNS-based traffic load balancer that enables administrators to distribute incoming traffic across

multiple Azure regions or endpoints based on various routing methods, including performance, priority, and geographic proximity. Administrators can configure Traffic Manager profiles and endpoints using the Azure CLI commands az network traffic-manager profile create and az network traffic-manager endpoint create, allowing them to implement redundancy and fault tolerance for their applications. Another crucial aspect of building highly available network infrastructures is implementing robust disaster recovery strategies. This involves replicating critical resources and data across geographically dispersed locations to ensure business continuity in the event of a disaster or outage. Azure Site Recovery is a disaster recovery as a service (DRaaS) offering that enables administrators to replicate VMs, applications, and data to Azure from on-premises datacenters or between Azure regions for failover and failback purposes. Administrators can configure Site Recovery protection using the Azure CLI commands az backup protection enable-for-vm for VMs or az backup protection enable-for-azurefileshare for Azure File Shares, specifying the source and target locations and replication settings. Additionally, Azure Backup provides backup and restore capabilities for Azure VMs, files, and applications, allowing administrators to protect critical data and workloads against accidental deletion, corruption, *or ransomware attacks. Administrators can configure backup policies and schedules using the Azure CLI commands az backup policy create and az backup protection enable, ensuring that data is regularly backed up and available for recovery when needed. In summary, building highly available network infrastructures in Azure requires a combination of redundant architectures, load balancing, traffic management, and disaster recovery strategies. By leveraging Azure services such as Virtual Machines, Load Balancer, Traffic Manager, Site Recovery, and Backup, administrators can design and deploy network infrastructures that provide uninterrupted connectivity, fault tolerance, and business continuity for their organizations.*

Chapter 3: Advanced Network Security Architecture with CLI

Implementing security best practices with the Azure Command-Line Interface (CLI) is essential for safeguarding cloud environments against various threats and vulnerabilities. One of the fundamental aspects of securing Azure resources is controlling access and permissions using Role-Based Access Control (RBAC). RBAC allows administrators to grant specific permissions to users, groups, or applications based on their roles, ensuring that only authorized entities have access to resources. With the Azure CLI, administrators can create custom RBAC roles with the necessary permissions using the az role definition create command, specifying the role name, description, and permissions. Once the custom role is defined, it can be assigned to users or groups using the az role assignment create command, associating the role with a specific scope such as a subscription, resource group, or resource. Another essential security best practice is implementing network security groups (NSGs) to control inbound and outbound traffic to Azure resources. NSGs act as virtual firewalls, allowing administrators to define security rules that permit or deny traffic based on source IP address, destination IP address, port, and protocol. Administrators can create NSGs using the az network nsg create command and then associate them with subnets or network interfaces using the az network vnet subnet update command or az network nic update command, respectively. By applying NSGs to resources, administrators can enforce network segmentation and restrict access to sensitive workloads. Encryption plays a crucial role in protecting data confidentiality and integrity both at rest and in transit. Azure Disk Encryption (ADE) enables administrators to encrypt OS and data disks attached to Azure Virtual Machines, ensuring that sensitive information is safeguarded against unauthorized access. ADE can be enabled using the az vm encryption enable command, specifying the VM name, resource group, and encryption settings such as encryption type and key vault details. Additionally, administrators can encrypt data stored in Azure Storage accounts using Azure Storage Service Encryption (SSE). SSE automatically encrypts data blobs at rest using Microsoft-managed keys, providing transparent encryption without requiring any changes to applications or workflows. SSE can be enabled at the storage account level using the az storage account update command with the --encryption-services blob parameter set to enabled. Secure access to Azure resources is paramount for preventing unauthorized access and data breaches. Azure Active Directory (AD) enables administrators to manage user identities and access to Azure resources centrally. With the Azure CLI, administrators can configure Azure AD settings, including user authentication methods, conditional access policies, and multi-factor authentication (MFA) settings. Azure AD authentication settings can be managed using the az ad sp credential reset command, allowing administrators to rotate service principal credentials regularly to enhance security. Additionally, administrators can enforce MFA for Azure AD users using the az ad user update command with the --force-change-password-next-login and --force-change-password-next-login parameters to require users to reset their passwords and enable MFA. Monitoring and auditing are critical components of a robust security strategy, allowing administrators to detect and respond to security incidents promptly. Azure Security Center provides a unified platform for monitoring the security posture of Azure resources, identifying potential threats, and implementing security recommendations. Administrators can use the Azure CLI to manage Security Center settings, including security policies, regulatory compliance, and threat detection configurations. The az security pricing create command can be used to enable Azure Defender for servers, enabling advanced threat protection for virtual machines, SQL databases, and containers. Additionally, administrators can configure security policies using the az security policy assignment create command, specifying the policy name, scope, and enforcement settings. In summary, implementing security best practices with the Azure CLI is essential for protecting Azure environments against cyber threats and ensuring compliance with industry regulations. By leveraging RBAC, NSGs, encryption, Azure AD, and Azure Security Center, administrators can establish robust security controls and mitigate security risks effectively. Advanced threat detection and prevention techniques are crucial components of modern cybersecurity strategies, especially in dynamic and evolving threat landscapes. Azure Security Center provides a comprehensive set of tools and features to help organizations detect, investigate, and respond to advanced threats effectively. One of the key capabilities of Azure Security Center is threat intelligence, which leverages global threat intelligence sources to identify and prioritize potential security risks. By analyzing vast amounts of security data and telemetry from Azure resources, Security Center can detect indicators of compromise (IOCs) and anomalous behavior that may indicate a security incident. Administrators can configure threat intelligence settings using the az security alert update command, specifying the alert name, resource group, and threat intelligence settings. Additionally, Security Center offers advanced behavioral analytics capabilities powered by machine learning algorithms. These algorithms analyze patterns of user and resource behavior to identify suspicious activities and potential security threats. By correlating multiple data sources and applying machine learning models, Security Center can detect threats such as *unauthorized access attempts, malware infections, and data exfiltration attempts. Administrators can enable behavioral analytics using the az security pricing create command, selecting the appropriate pricing tier and enabling advanced threat protection features. Another critical aspect of advanced threat detection is endpoint detection and response (EDR), which focuses on monitoring and responding to security incidents on individual endpoints such as servers and workstations. Azure Defender for Endpoints (formerly known as Microsoft Defender for Endpoint) integrates seamlessly with Azure Security Center to provide advanced EDR capabilities for Azure Virtual Machines and on-premises servers. Administrators can enable Azure Defender for Endpoints using the az security pricing create command, specifying the target resources and enabling endpoint protection features. Once enabled, Azure Defender for Endpoints continuously monitors endpoint activities, detects suspicious behavior, and responds to security incidents in real-time. Furthermore, Security Center offers integrated threat hunting capabilities, allowing security teams to proactively search for signs of compromise and potential security threats across Azure environments. Threat hunting involves analyzing security data, logs, and telemetry to identify hidden threats and malicious activities that may evade automated detection mechanisms. Security teams can conduct threat hunting exercises using the Security Center console or programmatically using the Azure CLI to execute queries and analyze results. By combining automated threat detection with proactive threat hunting, organizations can improve their overall security posture and reduce the risk of cyber attacks. Additionally, Security Center provides built-in incident response capabilities to help organizations respond to security incidents promptly and effectively. In the event of a security incident, administrators can initiate incident response actions directly from the Security Center console or using the Azure CLI commands. These actions may include isolating compromised resources, collecting forensic data for analysis, and remediating security vulnerabilities. By automating incident response processes and workflows, organizations can minimize the impact of security incidents and prevent further damage to their environments. In summary, advanced threat detection and prevention techniques are essential for protecting organizations against sophisticated cyber threats and ensuring the security and integrity of their Azure environments. By leveraging the advanced capabilities of Azure Security Center, including threat intelligence, behavioral analytics, endpoint detection and response, threat hunting, and incident response, organizations can detect, investigate, and respond to security threats effectively.*

Chapter 4: Implementing Multi-Region Network Deployments

Designing multi-region networking architectures requires careful consideration of various factors to ensure resilience, performance, and compliance across geographically distributed environments. One of the key considerations is selecting the appropriate network topology to connect resources across multiple regions effectively. Azure offers several networking options, including virtual networks (VNets), virtual network peering, and VPN gateways, which can be leveraged to establish secure and reliable connections between regions. Administrators can use the Azure CLI to create and manage virtual networks, peering connections, and VPN gateways, ensuring seamless connectivity between resources deployed in different regions. Another important aspect of multi-region networking design is implementing redundancy and fault tolerance to minimize the impact of region-specific outages or failures. This can be achieved by deploying redundant resources across multiple regions and leveraging Azure Traffic Manager to distribute traffic intelligently across healthy regions. By configuring Traffic Manager profiles using the az network traffic-manager profile create command and associating endpoints with different regions, administrators can achieve high availability and fault tolerance for their applications. Additionally, it's essential to consider network latency and performance when designing multi-region architectures. By deploying resources closer to end-users and leveraging Azure's global network infrastructure, organizations can reduce latency and improve the overall user experience. Azure's Content Delivery Network (CDN) can be used to cache content at edge locations worldwide, ensuring fast and reliable access to web applications and content regardless of the user's location. Administrators can configure CDN profiles and endpoints using the Azure CLI to optimize content delivery across multiple regions efficiently. Compliance and data sovereignty requirements are also critical considerations when designing multi-region networking architectures. Organizations must ensure that data residency and compliance regulations are met for each region where resources are deployed. Azure offers region-specific compliance certifications and data residency options, allowing organizations to choose the regions that best align with their regulatory requirements. Administrators can use the Azure CLI to specify the desired region when deploying resources, ensuring compliance with regional regulations and data sovereignty laws. Another important design consideration is implementing secure connectivity between regions to protect data in transit and prevent unauthorized access. Azure Virtual Network Gateways can be deployed to establish encrypted VPN connections between virtual networks in different regions, ensuring secure communication over the internet. By configuring VPN gateways using the az network vpn-gateway create command and defining connection settings, administrators can establish secure cross-region connectivity without compromising data security. Additionally, network segmentation and access control measures should be implemented to prevent lateral movement and unauthorized access within multi-region environments. Azure Network Security Groups (NSGs) can be used to define inbound and outbound traffic rules, restricting access to resources based on IP addresses, protocols, and ports. Administrators can manage NSG rules using the Azure CLI, ensuring granular control over network traffic within and between regions. Scalability and flexibility are also essential considerations for multi-region networking architectures, especially in dynamic and rapidly evolving environments. Azure offers scalable networking services such as Azure Load Balancer and Azure Application Gateway, which can be deployed across multiple regions to distribute traffic and scale applications horizontally. Administrators can use the Azure CLI to create and configure load balancer and application gateway resources, ensuring high availability and performance for multi-region applications. Additionally, automation and orchestration play a crucial role in managing and deploying multi-region networking architectures *efficiently. Azure Automation and Azure Resource Manager (ARM) templates can be used to automate the deployment and configuration of networking resources across multiple regions. By defining infrastructure as code and using tools like Azure DevOps and Git for version control, administrators can ensure consistency and repeatability in their multi-region deployments. In summary, designing multi-region networking architectures requires careful consideration of various factors, including network topology, redundancy, performance, compliance, security, scalability, and automation. By leveraging Azure's networking services and the Azure CLI, organizations can design and deploy resilient, high-performance, and compliant multi-region architectures that meet their business requirements and regulatory obligations effectively.*

Configuring cross-region connectivity is essential for organizations seeking to establish resilient and high-performing network architectures that span multiple geographic locations within the Azure cloud environment. Leveraging the Azure CLI, administrators can seamlessly deploy and manage the necessary networking components to facilitate cross-region connectivity. One of the primary methods for achieving cross-region connectivity is through the use of Azure Virtual Network (VNet) peering. VNet peering enables the establishment of private network connectivity between virtual networks deployed in different Azure regions, allowing resources within these VNets to communicate securely with one another. Using the Azure CLI, administrators can initiate the peering process by executing the az network vnet peering create command, specifying the source and destination VNets, as well as any additional configuration parameters such as peering names and resource group associations. Once the peering connections are established, traffic between resources in the peered VNets can traverse the Azure backbone network, ensuring low-latency communication and optimal performance. Another method for configuring cross-region connectivity is through the deployment of Azure Virtual Network Gateways. Virtual Network Gateways enable secure site-to-site or site-to-virtual network connectivity between on-premises networks and Azure VNets located in different regions. By deploying Virtual Network Gateways using the az network vpn-gateway create command, administrators can establish encrypted VPN tunnels across regions, providing a secure communication channel for cross-region traffic. Additionally, Virtual Network Gateways support high-availability configurations, ensuring continuous connectivity in the event of a gateway failure or region-specific outage. In scenarios where direct network peering or VPN connectivity is not feasible or practical, organizations can utilize Azure ExpressRoute to establish dedicated, private connections between their on-premises infrastructure and Azure data centers. ExpressRoute circuits can span multiple regions, allowing organizations to extend their private networks seamlessly across geographic boundaries. Administrators can provision ExpressRoute circuits and associated resources using the Azure CLI, specifying parameters such as circuit names, service providers, and bandwidth options with commands like az network express-route create. Once provisioned, ExpressRoute circuits provide dedicated, predictable, and low-latency connectivity for cross-region workloads, making them ideal for mission-critical applications and data-intensive workloads. Additionally, Azure offers a range of networking services and features that can enhance cross-region connectivity and address specific use cases or requirements. For example, Azure Traffic Manager enables global load balancing and traffic routing based on various criteria such as endpoint health, geographic proximity, or performance metrics. Administrators can configure Traffic Manager profiles and endpoints using the Azure CLI, ensuring optimal traffic distribution across regions for improved application availability and responsiveness. Similarly, Azure Front Door provides a scalable and secure global content delivery network (CDN) that optimizes web application delivery and accelerates content delivery to end-users worldwide. By deploying Front Door instances using the az network front-door create command, organizations can improve the performance, scalability, and availability of their *cross-region web applications and services. Additionally, Azure Firewall Manager enables centralized management and configuration of network security policies across multiple VNets and regions. Using the Azure CLI, administrators can deploy and configure Azure Firewall Manager policies to enforce consistent security controls and threat protection measures for cross-region traffic, safeguarding organizational assets and data from malicious activities and cyber threats. In summary, configuring cross-region connectivity with the Azure CLI empowers organizations to build robust, resilient, and high-performing network architectures that span multiple geographic locations within the Azure cloud environment. By leveraging networking services such as VNet peering, Virtual Network Gateways, ExpressRoute, Traffic Manager, Front Door, and Azure Firewall Manager, administrators can establish secure, reliable, and scalable connectivity across regions, enabling seamless communication and access to resources for distributed applications and workloads.*

Chapter 5: Optimizing Network Performance at Scale

Performance tuning strategies for large-scale networks are crucial for ensuring optimal operation and responsiveness, especially in environments where a multitude of resources and services are deployed across expansive network infrastructures. Leveraging the Azure CLI, administrators can implement various techniques to fine-tune the performance of their networks and enhance overall efficiency. One fundamental aspect of performance tuning is optimizing the configuration of virtual machines (VMs) and virtual networks (VNets) to accommodate large-scale workloads and traffic volumes. Administrators can use the az vm create command to provision VM instances with appropriate specifications, such as CPU cores, memory, and disk configurations, tailored to the requirements of specific applications or services. Additionally, optimizing network performance often involves optimizing the configuration of VNets, including subnet sizing, address space allocation, and routing configuration. By using the az network vnet create command, administrators can create VNets with optimal configurations, ensuring efficient routing and resource allocation within the network. Another crucial aspect of performance tuning is optimizing the allocation and utilization of resources such as storage and compute instances. Administrators can use the az monitor metrics list command to monitor resource utilization metrics, such as CPU usage, memory usage, and disk I/O, and identify potential bottlenecks or areas for optimization. Based on these metrics, administrators can adjust resource allocations, scale resources vertically or horizontally, or implement caching and optimization techniques to improve performance. Additionally, implementing load balancing solutions can help distribute incoming traffic evenly across multiple resources or instances, thereby improving overall network performance and availability. Administrators can use the az network lb create command to create Azure Load Balancer instances and configure them to distribute traffic across backend resources based on various load balancing algorithms, such as round-robin or least connections. Moreover, implementing content delivery networks (CDNs) can help optimize the delivery of content and reduce latency for distributed users and clients. Administrators can use the az cdn endpoint create command to create Azure CDN endpoints and configure them to cache content closer to end-users, thereby reducing latency and improving overall performance. Additionally, optimizing network security configurations can help improve performance by reducing the overhead associated with security measures such as encryption, authentication, and access control. Administrators can use the az network nsg rule create command to create network security group (NSG) rules and configure them to allow or deny traffic based on specific criteria, such as IP addresses, protocols, or port numbers. By implementing granular security policies and minimizing unnecessary traffic inspection, administrators can improve network performance without compromising security. Furthermore, implementing monitoring and analytics solutions can help administrators identify performance bottlenecks, troubleshoot issues, and optimize network configurations proactively. Administrators can use the az monitor metrics alert create command to create Azure Monitor alerts and configure them to notify administrators when predefined performance thresholds are exceeded. Additionally, administrators can use the az network watcher configure command to configure Azure Network Watcher, enabling network monitoring, diagnostics, and packet capture capabilities for proactive performance management and troubleshooting. In summary, performance tuning strategies for large-scale networks are essential for optimizing network performance, enhancing efficiency, and ensuring a seamless user experience. By leveraging the Azure CLI and implementing techniques such as optimizing resource configurations, implementing load balancing and CDN solutions, optimizing security configurations, and implementing monitoring and analytics solutions, administrators can effectively fine-tune the performance of their networks and meet the demands of large-scale *workloads and traffic volumes. Load balancing and traffic optimization techniques play a critical role in ensuring the availability, scalability, and performance of networked applications and services. These techniques are essential for distributing incoming network traffic across multiple servers or resources to prevent overloading and maximize resource utilization. One common method for implementing load balancing is through the use of a load balancer, which acts as an intermediary between clients and backend servers, distributing incoming requests based on predefined algorithms or rules. In Azure, administrators can create a load balancer using the az network lb create command, specifying parameters such as the frontend IP configuration, backend address pool, and load balancing rules. Additionally, administrators can configure load balancing rules to distribute traffic based on various criteria, such as round-robin, least connections, or source IP affinity, using the az network lb rule create command. Another approach to load balancing is the use of application delivery controllers (ADCs), which provide advanced traffic management features such as SSL termination, content caching, and application-layer routing. In Azure, administrators can deploy ADCs using virtual appliances from Azure Marketplace or third-party vendors, configuring them to distribute traffic across backend resources using the az vm create command to provision virtual machines and the appropriate networking configurations.*

Furthermore, administrators can leverage Azure Traffic Manager to implement DNS-based load balancing and global traffic management, directing users to the closest or most responsive endpoint based on factors such as geographic location, endpoint health, or performance metrics. By using the az network traffic-manager profile create command, administrators can create Traffic Manager profiles and configure them to route traffic to different endpoints using routing methods such as priority, weighted, or performance-based routing. Additionally, administrators can optimize traffic management and routing by implementing content delivery networks (CDNs) to cache and deliver content closer to end-users, reducing latency and improving overall performance. In Azure, administrators can create CDN endpoints using the az cdn endpoint create command, configuring them to cache and deliver content from origin servers or storage accounts to edge locations around the world. Moreover, administrators can use Azure Front Door to implement a global-scale, secure entry point for web applications, APIs, and content delivery, providing advanced traffic management features such as SSL offloading, DDoS protection, and intelligent routing based on real-time performance metrics. By using the az network front-door create command, administrators can create Front Door instances and configure them to route traffic to different backend pools or endpoints based on various criteria such as URL path, hostname, or geographic location. Additionally, administrators can optimize traffic performance by implementing caching and compression techniques to reduce bandwidth usage and improve response times. In Azure, administrators can enable content caching for web applications or APIs using features such as Azure CDN or Azure Front Door, configuring caching rules and policies to cache static content or dynamic content with appropriate cache-control headers. Furthermore, administrators can implement HTTP compression using features such as Azure Application Gateway or third-party ADCs, configuring compression settings to compress HTTP responses before they are sent to clients, reducing bandwidth usage and improving page load times. Additionally, administrators can optimize traffic performance by implementing QoS (Quality of Service) configurations to prioritize network traffic based on predefined criteria such as application type, user role, or business priority. In Azure, administrators can configure QoS policies using features such as Azure Firewall, Azure Application Gateway, or Azure Virtual WAN, specifying parameters such as bandwidth limits, latency thresholds, or packet prioritization rules to ensure optimal performance for critical applications or services. Moreover, administrators can monitor and analyze network traffic using tools such as Azure Monitor, Azure Network Watcher, or third-party monitoring solutions to identify performance bottlenecks, troubleshoot issues, and optimize traffic management configurations proactively. By using the az monitor metrics list command, administrators can retrieve performance metrics such as network latency, throughput, or error rates, analyzing them to identify trends or anomalies that may indicate underlying issues or opportunities for optimization. Additionally, administrators can use the az network watcher packet-capture create command to capture network packets for analysis, inspecting packet headers and payloads to diagnose connectivity issues, protocol errors, or performance bottlenecks. Furthermore, administrators can use the az network watcher flow-log configure command to configure flow logging for network interfaces or resources, capturing detailed information about inbound and outbound traffic flows, including source and destination IP addresses, ports, and protocols. Overall, load balancing and traffic optimization techniques are essential for ensuring the availability, scalability, and performance of networked applications and services in cloud environments. By leveraging Azure CLI commands and features such as load balancers, traffic managers, content delivery networks, caching and compression, QoS configurations, and network monitoring tools, administrators can optimize traffic management and routing, reduce latency, and improve overall user experience.

Chapter 6: Advanced Network Automation and Orchestration Techniques

Orchestrating network deployments with CLI tools is an essential aspect of managing complex network infrastructures efficiently and effectively in cloud environments. By leveraging CLI commands and automation scripts, administrators can streamline the process of provisioning, configuring, and managing network resources, reducing manual errors and increasing deployment consistency. One fundamental aspect of orchestrating network deployments with CLI is the use of infrastructure as code (IaC) principles, which involve defining network configurations and deployments in machine-readable scripts or templates. In Azure, administrators can use Azure Resource Manager (ARM) templates to define the desired state of Azure resources, including virtual networks, subnets, security groups, and routing tables, using JSON or YAML syntax. By using the az deployment group create command, administrators can deploy ARM templates to Azure subscriptions or resource groups, specifying parameters such as the template file, resource group name, and deployment parameters. Additionally, administrators can leverage Azure CLI commands to automate the process of creating and configuring virtual networks and subnets, which are foundational components of network deployments. For example, administrators can use the az network vnet create command to create a virtual network, specifying parameters such as the resource group, name, address space, and subnet configurations. Similarly, administrators can use the az network vnet subnet create command to create subnets within a virtual network, specifying parameters such as the subnet name, address prefix, and virtual network name. Moreover, administrators can use Azure CLI commands to automate the configuration of network security groups (NSGs), which are used to control inbound and outbound traffic to network resources based on security rules. For example, administrators can use the az network nsg create command to create an NSG, specifying parameters such as the resource group, name, and location. Subsequently, administrators can use the az network nsg rule create command to define security rules for the NSG, specifying parameters such as the rule name, priority, source and destination IP addresses, ports, and protocols. Additionally, administrators can orchestrate network deployments with CLI tools by integrating with configuration management and automation frameworks such as Ansible, Terraform, or Puppet. These tools provide higher-level abstractions and workflow automation capabilities for managing network configurations and deployments across multiple cloud platforms and environments. For example, administrators can use Ansible playbooks to define network configurations and deployment tasks, leveraging Azure CLI modules to interact with Azure resources programmatically. Similarly, administrators can use Terraform configurations to define network infrastructure as code, using the Azure provider to provision and manage Azure resources using CLI commands under the hood. Furthermore, administrators can leverage Azure CLI commands to orchestrate the deployment of network monitoring and logging solutions, which are essential for ensuring the security, performance, and compliance of network infrastructures. For example, administrators can use the az monitor log-analytics workspace create command to create a Log Analytics workspace, which collects and analyzes telemetry data from network resources. Subsequently, administrators can use the az monitor diagnostic-settings create command to configure diagnostic settings for Azure resources, specifying parameters such as the resource type, logs, and metrics to be collected and stored in the Log Analytics workspace. Overall, orchestrating network deployments with CLI tools enables administrators to automate and streamline the process of provisioning, configuring, and managing network resources in cloud environments. By leveraging CLI commands, automation scripts, and infrastructure as code principles, administrators can achieve greater consistency, reliability, and scalability in their network deployments, ultimately improving operational efficiency and agility.

Automating network provisioning and configuration is an essential aspect of modern IT operations, enabling organizations to achieve greater efficiency, scalability, and consistency in managing their network infrastructure. One of the key techniques for automating network provisioning and configuration is leveraging infrastructure as code (IaC) principles, which involve defining and managing network resources using machine-readable scripts or templates. In cloud environments like Azure, administrators can use tools like Azure CLI or Azure PowerShell to automate the provisioning and configuration of network resources. For example, using Azure CLI, administrators can create virtual networks, subnets, network security groups, and other network components using simple command-line commands. The az network vnet create command can be used to create a virtual network, specifying parameters such as the resource group, name, address space, and location. Similarly, the az network vnet subnet create command can be used to create subnets within the virtual network, specifying parameters such as the subnet name, address prefix, and virtual network name. Additionally, administrators can automate the configuration of network security groups (NSGs) using commands like az network nsg create and az network nsg rule create to create NSGs and define security rules respectively. By automating network provisioning and configuration using CLI commands, organizations can significantly reduce the time and effort required to deploy and manage their network infrastructure. Another technique for automating network provisioning and configuration is using configuration management tools like Ansible, Puppet, or Chef. These tools provide higher-level abstractions and workflow automation capabilities for managing network configurations across multiple devices and environments. For example, Ansible playbooks can be used to define network configurations and deploy them to a fleet of devices simultaneously. Ansible uses SSH to connect to network devices and execute configuration commands, making it a versatile tool for automating network provisioning and configuration tasks. Similarly, Puppet and Chef use agent-based architectures to enforce desired configurations on network devices, ensuring consistency and compliance across the infrastructure. Moreover, organizations can leverage version control systems like Git to manage their network automation scripts and templates, enabling collaboration, versioning, and rollback capabilities. By storing network automation code in version control repositories, organizations can track changes, collaborate with team members, and revert to previous configurations if necessary. Furthermore, organizations can integrate network automation into their continuous integration/continuous deployment (CI/CD) pipelines to automate the testing and deployment of network configurations. By *incorporating network automation scripts and templates into CI/CD workflows, organizations can ensure that network changes are thoroughly tested and deployed in a controlled and repeatable manner. Additionally, organizations can use tools like Azure DevOps or Jenkins to orchestrate the execution of network automation tasks, triggering deployments based on predefined conditions or events. By automating network provisioning and configuration, organizations can achieve several benefits, including faster time to market, reduced risk of human error, improved scalability, and greater agility in responding to changing business requirements. Overall, automation is a key enabler for modernizing network operations and driving digital transformation initiatives within organizations.*

Chapter 7: Designing for High Availability and Disaster Recovery

Implementing disaster recovery strategies with CLI commands is crucial for ensuring the resilience and continuity of business operations in the face of unexpected disruptions or outages. One of the primary techniques for implementing disaster recovery is through the replication of critical resources and data to a secondary location, commonly referred to as a disaster recovery site. In Azure, administrators can use Azure CLI to configure and manage disaster recovery solutions for various Azure services. For example, Azure Site Recovery (ASR) is a comprehensive disaster recovery service that enables organizations to replicate virtual machines, applications, and workloads from on-premises environments or other Azure regions to a secondary Azure region. Using Azure CLI, administrators can initiate the replication of virtual machines to a target Azure region using commands like az backup protection enable-for-vm and az backup protection auto-enable-for-vm, which enable backup protection for virtual machines and automatically enable backup protection for new virtual machines respectively. Additionally, administrators can use commands like az backup protection recoverypoint list and az backup restore restore-disks to list recovery points for virtual machines and initiate the restoration of virtual machine disks from recovery points respectively. Another disaster recovery technique is to leverage Azure Storage replication options to replicate critical data across Azure regions for redundancy and data durability. Azure Storage provides several replication options, including Locally Redundant Storage (LRS), Zone-Redundant Storage (ZRS), Geo-Redundant Storage (GRS), and Read-Access Geo-Redundant Storage (RA-GRS). Using Azure CLI, administrators can configure storage accounts with the desired replication options to ensure data resilience and availability across multiple Azure regions. For example, the az storage account create command can be used to create a storage account with the specified replication type, such as GRS or RA-GRS, ensuring that data is replicated to a secondary region for disaster recovery purposes. Additionally, administrators can use Azure CLI to automate the failover process in the event of a disaster, ensuring minimal downtime and data loss. For example, using Azure CLI, administrators can trigger the failover of virtual machines or applications from the primary region to the secondary region using commands like az vm disaster-recovery failover or az sql db replication failover, depending on the type of resource being failed over. Furthermore, administrators can use Azure CLI to monitor the health and status of disaster recovery resources and configurations, enabling proactive management and troubleshooting. For example, the az vm disaster-recovery show command can be used to display the status of virtual machine replication and failover configurations, providing insights into the current state of disaster recovery operations. By implementing disaster recovery strategies with CLI commands, organizations can enhance their resilience to disruptions and minimize the impact of outages on business operations. With the ability to automate replication, failover, and monitoring tasks, administrators can ensure that critical resources and data are protected and available when needed, enabling business continuity in the face of adversity.

Failover and redundancy planning for high availability is a critical aspect of ensuring the resilience and continuity of business operations in the event of unexpected disruptions or outages. One of the primary techniques for achieving high availability is through the implementation of failover mechanisms and redundancy architectures. Failover refers to the process of automatically switching to a standby system or resource when the primary system or resource becomes unavailable or fails. Redundancy, on the other hand, involves the duplication of critical components or systems to ensure that there are backup resources available in case of failure. In the context of IT infrastructure and networks, failover and redundancy planning typically involves the deployment of redundant hardware, software, and network configurations to eliminate single points of *failure and minimize downtime. One common approach to implementing failover and redundancy is through the use of load balancers and clustering technologies. Load balancers distribute incoming network traffic across multiple servers or resources, ensuring that no single server becomes overwhelmed and improving overall reliability and performance. For example, in Azure, administrators can use Azure Load Balancer to distribute incoming traffic across multiple virtual machines or services, ensuring high availability and fault tolerance. Using Azure CLI, administrators can configure and manage Azure Load Balancer settings, including backend pools, health probes, and traffic rules, to optimize performance and resilience. Additionally, administrators can leverage clustering technologies such as Windows Server Failover Clustering (WSFC) or Linux High Availability (HA) Clustering to create clusters of servers or virtual machines that work together to provide failover support and redundancy. These clusters can automatically detect and respond to failures by transferring workloads to healthy nodes within the cluster, minimizing downtime and ensuring continuous availability of services. Using Azure CLI, administrators can deploy and configure clusters of virtual machines for high availability scenarios, ensuring that critical workloads remain operational even in the event of hardware or software failures. Furthermore, administrators can implement database replication and synchronization techniques to ensure data availability and consistency in high availability environments. For example, Azure SQL Database offers built-in support for database replication and failover, allowing administrators to configure geo-replication for automatic failover to a secondary region in case of a primary region failure. Using Azure CLI, administrators can enable geo-replication for Azure SQL Database instances and configure failover policies to ensure data integrity and availability across regions. Another important aspect of failover and redundancy planning is the implementation of backup and recovery strategies to protect against data loss and ensure business continuity. Administrators can use Azure CLI to automate the backup and recovery of critical data and resources, including virtual machines, databases, and storage accounts. For example, the az backup policy create command can be used to create backup policies for virtual machines, specifying the backup frequency, retention period, and other settings. Additionally, administrators can use Azure CLI to initiate backup and recovery operations, monitor backup jobs, and perform disaster recovery tests to validate the effectiveness of their failover and redundancy strategies. By implementing failover and redundancy planning with CLI commands, organizations can enhance the availability, reliability, and resilience of their IT infrastructure and networks, ensuring uninterrupted access to critical resources and services in the face of disruptions and outages.*

Chapter 8: Network Cost Optimization Strategies

Cost optimization is a critical aspect of managing Azure networking resources efficiently and ensuring that organizations derive maximum value from their investments in the cloud. There are several best practices and techniques that organizations can employ to optimize costs while maintaining the performance, scalability, and reliability of their Azure networking infrastructure. One of the fundamental principles of cost optimization is rightsizing resources to match workload requirements. This involves selecting the appropriate instance types, sizes, and configurations for virtual machines, databases, and other networking components based on workload characteristics, performance benchmarks, and usage patterns. By rightsizing resources, organizations can avoid over-provisioning and underutilization, which can lead to unnecessary costs. Azure provides several tools and features to help organizations analyze resource utilization and identify opportunities for rightsizing. For example, Azure Advisor offers recommendations for rightsizing virtual machines, storage accounts, and other resources based on historical usage data and performance metrics. By following Azure Advisor recommendations and adjusting resource configurations accordingly, organizations can optimize costs without sacrificing performance or reliability. Another key aspect of cost optimization is leveraging Azure Reserved Instances (RI) and Azure Hybrid Benefit (AHB) to reduce compute and networking costs. Reserved Instances allow organizations to pre-purchase virtual machine instances for a one- or three-year term at significantly discounted rates compared to pay-as-you-go pricing. By committing to Reserved Instances for predictable workloads, organizations can achieve substantial cost savings over the long term. Additionally, Azure Hybrid Benefit enables organizations with on-premises licenses to use their existing Windows Server and SQL Server licenses to run virtual machines and databases in Azure at discounted rates. By taking advantage of Azure Hybrid Benefit, organizations can reduce licensing costs and optimize their overall cloud expenditure. Azure Cost Management + Billing provides insights into cloud spending and helps organizations track, analyze, and optimize costs across Azure services. With Azure Cost Management, organizations can set budgets, create alerts for cost overruns, and identify opportunities for cost savings through rightsizing, reservation purchases, and workload optimization. Additionally, Azure Cost Management provides recommendations for cost optimization based on usage patterns and cost trends, helping organizations implement proactive cost-saving measures. By regularly monitoring and analyzing cloud spending with Azure Cost Management, organizations can identify cost optimization opportunities and make informed decisions to control and reduce their Azure networking costs. Another cost optimization best practice is to leverage serverless computing services such as Azure Functions and Azure Logic Apps for lightweight, event-driven workloads. Serverless computing eliminates the need to provision and manage infrastructure, allowing organizations to pay only for the compute resources consumed during the execution of functions or workflows. By using serverless services, organizations can reduce operational overhead and infrastructure costs associated with traditional virtual machines or containers. Additionally, organizations can take advantage of Azure networking features such as Azure Virtual WAN and Azure ExpressRoute to optimize connectivity and reduce data transfer costs between on-premises data centers and Azure regions. Virtual WAN enables organizations to connect multiple branch offices and data centers to Azure using a centralized hub-and-spoke architecture, reducing the need for costly site-to-site VPN or MPLS connections. ExpressRoute provides dedicated, private connectivity between on-premises networks and Azure, offering lower latency, higher bandwidth, and predictable data transfer costs compared to public internet connections. By leveraging Virtual WAN and ExpressRoute, organizations can optimize network performance and reduce data egress costs associated with hybrid cloud deployments. Additionally, organizations can use Azure Traffic Manager and Azure CDN to optimize the delivery of web applications and content to users around the world. Traffic Manager enables global load balancing and traffic routing based on user proximity, endpoint health, and other configurable rules, ensuring optimal performance and availability for distributed applications. CDN caches static content at edge locations worldwide, reducing latency and bandwidth usage for content delivery to end users. By implementing Traffic Manager and CDN, organizations can improve the user experience and reduce data transfer costs associated with serving content to global audiences. In summary, cost optimization is a continuous process that requires proactive monitoring, analysis, and optimization of Azure networking resources. By following best practices such as rightsizing resources, leveraging Reserved Instances and Hybrid Benefit, using serverless computing, optimizing connectivity with Virtual WAN and ExpressRoute, and utilizing Traffic Manager and CDN, organizations can effectively manage and reduce their Azure networking costs while maintaining performance, scalability, and reliability. Monitoring and managing network costs is a crucial aspect of cloud infrastructure management, particularly in Azure, where resources are billed based on usage. Azure provides various tools and features to help organizations monitor and manage their network costs effectively using the command-line interface (CLI). One of the fundamental CLI commands for monitoring network costs in Azure is the az monitor command, which enables users to retrieve and analyze cost-related metrics and logs. For example, you can use the az monitor metrics list command to list available metrics for a specific resource or resource group, including metrics related to network usage, data transfer, and resource consumption. By analyzing these metrics, organizations can gain insights into their network costs and identify areas for optimization. Additionally, the az monitor log-analytics command allows users to query and analyze log data collected by Azure Monitor, including network-related logs such as traffic flow logs, security logs, and diagnostic logs. By querying log data using the Kusto Query Language (KQL), organizations can filter, aggregate, and visualize network-related events and anomalies, helping them identify cost-saving opportunities and optimize network performance. Another useful CLI command for monitoring network costs in Azure is the az network watcher command, which provides tools and features for network monitoring, troubleshooting, and optimization. For example, you can use the az network watcher flow-log command to enable flow logs for virtual networks, subnets, or network interfaces, allowing you to capture and analyze network traffic for billing purposes. By analyzing flow logs using Azure Monitor or third-party log analysis tools, organizations can gain insights into their network usage patterns, identify anomalies and inefficiencies, and optimize network costs accordingly. Additionally, the az network watcher packet-capture command enables users to capture and analyze network packets in real-time, allowing them to troubleshoot network issues, monitor network performance, and optimize network costs by identifying and resolving inefficiencies and bottlenecks. By capturing packet data using Azure Network Watcher and analyzing it using packet analysis tools, organizations can gain granular visibility into their network traffic and identify opportunities for optimization. Azure Cost Management + Billing provides comprehensive insights into cloud spending, including network costs, and allows organizations to track, analyze, and optimize their network costs using the CLI. For example, you can use the az consumption usage list command to list usage data for Azure services, *including network-related services such as virtual networks, VPN gateways, and data transfer. By analyzing usage data and cost trends using Azure Cost Management, organizations can identify cost-saving opportunities, set budgets and alerts for cost overruns, and optimize their network spending effectively. Additionally, Azure Cost Management provides recommendations for cost optimization based on usage patterns, resource configurations, and cost-saving opportunities, helping organizations implement proactive cost-saving measures and optimize their network costs continuously. Another important aspect of monitoring and managing network costs in Azure is understanding the pricing model and cost factors associated with Azure networking services. Azure provides detailed documentation and pricing calculators to help organizations estimate and forecast their network costs accurately. By understanding the pricing model and cost factors for Azure networking services such as virtual networks, VPN gateways, and data transfer, organizations can make informed decisions about resource provisioning, deployment architectures, and cost optimization strategies to minimize their network costs effectively. Furthermore, organizations can leverage Azure Cost Management APIs and PowerShell scripts to automate cost monitoring and management tasks, enabling them to programmatically retrieve, analyze, and optimize their network costs using the CLI. By integrating Azure Cost Management APIs with custom monitoring and reporting solutions, organizations can gain real-time visibility into their network spending, implement cost-saving policies and recommendations, and optimize their network costs proactively. In summary, monitoring and managing network costs in Azure is essential for organizations to optimize their cloud spending, maximize their return on investment, and ensure cost-efficient operation of their cloud infrastructure. By leveraging CLI commands, tools, and features such as Azure Monitor, Azure Network Watcher, and Azure Cost Management, organizations can gain visibility into their network usage, analyze cost-related metrics and logs, identify cost-saving opportunities, and implement proactive cost optimization strategies effectively.*

Chapter 9: Compliance and Governance in Azure Networking

Implementing compliance standards is a critical aspect of maintaining the security and integrity of an organization's infrastructure, and leveraging the command-line interface (CLI) in cloud environments like Azure can streamline this process. Azure Policy is a powerful tool that allows administrators to enforce compliance standards and governance policies across their Azure subscriptions. Using the az policy command, administrators can create, assign, and manage policies that define specific rules and requirements for resource configurations, access controls, and security settings. For example, the az policy definition create command enables administrators to define custom policy rules based on regulatory standards such as HIPAA, GDPR, or PCI DSS, as well as organizational policies and best practices. These policy rules can include requirements for encryption, access controls, data retention, and other security measures to ensure compliance with industry regulations and internal guidelines. Once policy definitions are created, they can be assigned to Azure subscriptions, resource groups, or individual resources using the az policy assignment command. By assigning policies to specific scopes, administrators can enforce compliance standards across their Azure environment and automatically remediate non-compliant resources. For example, administrators can use the az policy assignment create command to assign a policy definition to a subscription, ensuring that all resources deployed within that subscription adhere to the specified compliance requirements. Azure Policy also provides built-in policy definitions for common compliance standards such as Azure CIS Benchmarks, NIST SP 800-53, and ISO 27001. These built-in policies can be deployed using the az policy command or through the Azure portal, allowing administrators to quickly and easily enforce compliance standards without the need for custom policy definitions. In addition to Azure Policy, administrators can use other CLI tools and features to implement compliance standards in their Azure environment. For example, the az keyvault command enables administrators to create and manage Azure Key Vaults, which can be used to store and manage cryptographic keys, secrets, and certificates. By storing sensitive information such as encryption keys and connection strings in Azure Key Vault, organizations can ensure that data is protected according to compliance requirements and industry best practices. Similarly, the az security command provides tools and features for managing security-related configurations and settings in Azure. Administrators can use commands such as az security compliance, az security recommendation, and az security contact to monitor compliance status, view security recommendations, and manage security contacts for Azure subscriptions. These tools enable administrators to identify potential security risks, address compliance gaps, and maintain a secure and compliant Azure environment. Another important aspect of implementing compliance standards with CLI is automating compliance checks and remediation tasks. Administrators can use scripting languages such as PowerShell or Bash to create custom automation scripts that perform compliance checks, enforce policy requirements, and remediate non-compliant resources automatically. By integrating these scripts with Azure Automation, Azure Functions, or other automation services, organizations can ensure continuous compliance monitoring and enforcement across their Azure environment. Additionally, administrators can leverage Azure Policy's built-in remediation tasks to automatically correct non-compliant resources based on policy definitions. For example, administrators can configure policy definitions to audit resources for compliance violations and automatically remediate non-compliant configurations using Azure Automation runbooks or custom scripts. By combining these automation capabilities with CLI commands, organizations can streamline compliance management processes, reduce manual intervention, and ensure consistent enforcement of compliance standards across their Azure environment. In summary, implementing compliance standards with CLI is essential for organizations to maintain a secure, compliant, and well-governed Azure environment. By leveraging tools such as Azure Policy, Azure Key Vault, and Azure Security Center, administrators can define, enforce, and automate compliance requirements according to regulatory standards, industry best practices, and organizational policies. Through CLI commands and automation scripts, organizations can streamline compliance management processes, reduce manual effort, and ensure continuous compliance monitoring and enforcement in their Azure environment. Enforcing governance policies for Azure networks is crucial for maintaining security, compliance, and operational efficiency within an organization's cloud infrastructure. Azure Policy is a key tool for enforcing governance policies across Azure networks. With Azure Policy, administrators can define and enforce rules that govern various aspects of network configurations, such as security, access controls, resource tagging, and naming conventions. Using the az policy command, administrators can create, assign, and manage policies to ensure that Azure resources deployed within the network adhere to organizational standards and compliance requirements. For example, administrators can use the az policy definition create command to create custom policy definitions that specify the desired governance rules for network configurations. These policy definitions can include requirements for network security groups (NSGs), virtual network (VNet) configurations, routing rules, and other network-related settings. Once the policy definitions are created, administrators can use the az policy assignment create command to assign them to specific Azure subscriptions, resource groups, or individual resources. By assigning policies at different scopes, administrators can enforce governance policies across the entire Azure network or specific subsets of resources. Azure Policy also provides built-in policy definitions that cover common governance requirements, such as requiring resource tags, restricting public IP addresses, and enforcing encryption settings. These built-in policies can be deployed using the az policy command or through the Azure portal, making it easy for administrators to implement governance policies without the need for custom definitions. In addition to Azure Policy, administrators can use other CLI commands and features to enforce governance policies for Azure networks. For example, the az network command provides a wide range of capabilities for managing Azure network resources, including VNets, subnets, NSGs, and route tables. Administrators can use commands such as az network vnet create, az network nsg create, and az network route-table create to provision and configure network resources according to governance requirements. By leveraging these commands, administrators can ensure that network configurations align with organizational standards and compliance requirements. Another important aspect of enforcing governance policies for

Azure networks is continuous monitoring and compliance reporting. Administrators can use the az monitor command to monitor network traffic, analyze security logs, and generate compliance reports. For example, the az monitor log-analytics workspace command enables administrators to create Log Analytics workspaces for collecting and analyzing network telemetry data. Administrators can then use the az monitor metrics alert command to set up alerts for detecting security incidents or policy violations within the Azure network. By monitoring network activity and compliance status, administrators can identify potential risks and take proactive measures to address them. Automation is another key component of enforcing governance policies for Azure networks. Administrators can use scripting languages such as PowerShell or Bash to create automation scripts that enforce governance policies, remediate non-compliant resources, and generate compliance reports. For example, administrators can use Azure Automation to schedule scripts that scan network configurations for compliance violations and automatically remediate any non-compliant settings. By integrating these automation scripts with Azure Policy, administrators can ensure consistent enforcement of governance policies across the Azure network. In summary, enforcing governance policies for Azure networks is essential for maintaining security, compliance, and operational efficiency within an organization's cloud infrastructure. By leveraging Azure Policy, CLI commands, monitoring tools, and automation capabilities, administrators can define, enforce, and monitor governance rules that govern network configurations and ensure compliance with organizational standards and regulatory requirements. Through continuous monitoring, reporting, and automation, administrators can proactively manage network security and compliance posture, reducing risks and improving overall governance of Azure networks.

Chapter 10: Managing and Scaling Complex Network Infrastructures

Managing network complexity with CLI tools is a fundamental aspect of network administration in modern IT environments, where networks are becoming increasingly intricate and diverse. CLI tools provide administrators with powerful capabilities to configure, monitor, and troubleshoot network infrastructure efficiently. One of the primary challenges in network management is dealing with the complexity arising from the proliferation of devices, services, and configurations within the network. CLI tools, such as PowerShell and Bash, offer administrators a command-line interface to interact with network devices, services, and configurations in a streamlined and scriptable manner. For example, administrators can use the az network command in Azure CLI to manage various aspects of Azure networking, including virtual networks, subnets, network security groups, and route tables. Similarly, in on-premises environments, administrators can use tools like Cisco IOS CLI, Juniper Junos CLI, or PowerShell Remoting to manage routers, switches, and other network devices. These CLI tools provide administrators with granular control over network configurations, allowing them to configure settings such as IP addresses, VLANs, routing protocols, and access control lists (ACLs) with precision. In addition to configuration management, CLI tools also play a crucial role in network monitoring and troubleshooting. Administrators can use CLI commands to collect real-time performance data, monitor network traffic, and diagnose connectivity issues. For example, the ping command can be used to test network connectivity between devices by sending ICMP echo requests and receiving ICMP echo replies. Similarly, the traceroute command can be used to trace the path that packets take from the source to the destination, helping administrators identify network hops and potential bottlenecks. CLI tools also provide capabilities for troubleshooting network security issues. Administrators can use commands like nslookup to query DNS servers and resolve domain names to IP addresses, netstat to display network connections and routing tables, and tcpdump to capture and analyze network packets. By leveraging these CLI tools, administrators can identify security vulnerabilities, detect suspicious network activity, and implement appropriate countermeasures to mitigate security risks. Another aspect of managing network complexity with CLI tools is automation. CLI tools enable administrators to automate repetitive tasks, streamline workflows, and improve operational efficiency. For example, administrators can use scripting languages like PowerShell or Bash to create automation scripts that perform routine network management tasks, such as configuring VLANs, deploying firewall rules, or provisioning virtual machines. These scripts can be scheduled to run automatically or triggered in response to specific events, reducing the need for manual intervention and minimizing the risk of human error. Furthermore, CLI tools support version control and configuration management practices, allowing administrators to track changes to network configurations, revert to previous states if necessary, and ensure consistency across the network infrastructure. By storing configuration files in version control systems like Git and using tools like Ansible or Puppet for configuration management, administrators can maintain a centralized repository of network configurations, enforce configuration standards, and facilitate collaboration among team members. In summary, managing network complexity with CLI tools is essential for effective network administration in modern IT environments. CLI tools provide administrators with the flexibility, control, and automation capabilities needed to configure, monitor, and troubleshoot complex network infrastructures. By leveraging CLI commands, scripting languages, automation frameworks, and configuration management practices, *administrators can streamline network management workflows, improve operational efficiency, and ensure the reliability, security, and performance of their network infrastructure. Strategies for scaling and growing network infrastructures are essential components of modern IT management, particularly as organizations expand, adopt new technologies, and accommodate increasing demands on their networks. One crucial aspect of scaling network infrastructures is the ability to accommodate growth in terms of users, devices, applications, and data traffic. To achieve this, organizations often employ various strategies, including vertical and horizontal scaling, network segmentation, and the adoption of scalable network technologies. Vertical scaling involves increasing the capacity of individual network components, such as servers, routers, or switches, to handle larger workloads. For example, administrators can add more memory, CPU cores, or storage to servers to improve their processing power and storage capacity. Similarly, network devices like routers and switches can be upgraded to higher-performance models with greater throughput and port density. Vertical scaling can help organizations meet immediate capacity requirements but may not be sufficient for long-term growth, especially when dealing with exponential increases in network traffic or the addition of large numbers of users or devices.*

Horizontal scaling, on the other hand, involves adding more instances of network components to distribute workloads across multiple devices. For example, organizations can deploy multiple servers in a load-balanced configuration to handle increased web traffic or implement redundant routers and switches to improve network reliability and fault tolerance. Horizontal scaling provides greater scalability and resilience than vertical scaling and is well-suited for accommodating unpredictable growth and ensuring high availability. Another strategy for scaling network infrastructures is network segmentation, which involves dividing a large network into smaller, isolated segments or subnets. By segmenting the network, organizations can improve performance, security, and manageability by reducing broadcast domains, limiting the scope of network traffic, and enforcing access controls between different parts of the network. For example, organizations can segment their network into separate VLANs (Virtual Local Area Networks) based on department, function, or security requirements and use routers or firewalls to control traffic between VLANs. Additionally, organizations can deploy software-defined networking (SDN) technologies to dynamically manage network segmentation and traffic routing based on application or user requirements. Cloud-based network services and virtualization *technologies also play a significant role in scaling and growing network infrastructures. Organizations can leverage cloud platforms like AWS, Azure, or Google Cloud to offload network services, such as load balancing, content delivery, and security, to scalable and resilient cloud-based infrastructure. Virtualization technologies, such as virtual machines (VMs), containers, and virtual networks, enable organizations to abstract and pool network resources, making it easier to scale and manage network infrastructure in dynamic and rapidly changing environments. Additionally, organizations can use container orchestration platforms like Kubernetes to automate the deployment, scaling, and management of containerized applications across distributed networks. Monitoring and analytics tools are essential for scaling and growing network infrastructures effectively. By collecting and analyzing network performance data, organizations can identify bottlenecks, predict capacity requirements, and optimize network resources to meet changing demands. For example, organizations can use network monitoring tools like Nagios, Zabbix, or Prometheus to monitor network traffic, bandwidth utilization, latency, and packet loss in real-time and proactively address performance issues before they impact users. Similarly, organizations can leverage network analytics platforms like Cisco DNA Center, Arista*

CloudVision, or Juniper Mist to gain insights into network traffic patterns, application performance, and user behavior and use this information to optimize network configurations and improve service delivery. In summary, scaling and growing network infrastructures require a combination of strategies, technologies, and tools to accommodate increasing demands, ensure high performance, and maintain reliability and security. By employing vertical and horizontal scaling, network segmentation, cloud-based services, virtualization technologies, and monitoring and analytics tools, organizations can effectively scale their network infrastructures to meet the evolving needs of their users and applications in a rapidly changing digital landscape.

Conclusion

In summary, the "Azure Networking Command Line Mastery" book bundle offers a comprehensive journey from beginner to architect level proficiency in managing Azure networking environments using the Command Line Interface (CLI). Through the four books included in this bundle, readers gain a solid foundation in Azure networking essentials, intermediate techniques, advanced optimization strategies, and expert-level best practices.

In Book 1, "Azure Networking Essentials: A Beginner's Guide to Command Line Basics," readers are introduced to the fundamentals of Azure networking and learn how to navigate the Azure CLI to perform basic networking tasks. They acquire essential skills such as creating virtual networks, subnets, and network security groups.

Building on this foundation, Book 2, "Mastering Azure CLI: Intermediate Techniques for Networking in the Cloud," delves deeper into intermediate-level techniques for managing Azure networking resources. Readers learn advanced networking concepts such as implementing virtual network peering, configuring Azure DNS, and deploying virtual network gateways.

In Book 3, "Advanced Azure Networking: Optimizing Performance and Security with CLI Mastery," readers explore advanced optimization strategies and security best practices for Azure networking. They discover techniques for optimizing network performance, implementing granular security policies, and leveraging advanced features like Azure Firewall and Application Gateway.

Finally, Book 4, "Azure Networking Architect: Expert Strategies and Best Practices for CLI Power Users," equips readers with expert-level strategies and best practices for designing and architecting Azure networking solutions. Readers learn how to design redundant and highly available network architectures, implement advanced traffic management and routing techniques, and enforce governance policies for Azure networks.

Collectively, this book bundle provides a comprehensive roadmap for mastering Azure networking through CLI mastery, from beginner to architect level proficiency. Whether you are just starting your journey in Azure networking or aiming to become a CLI power user and network architect, this bundle equips you with the knowledge and skills needed to succeed in managing and optimizing Azure networking environments at scale.